Ronald Harwood was born in C
He was Visitor in Theatre at Ba
has been president of English PEN since 1989.

REFLECTED GLORY

Ronald Harwood

faber and faber

LONDON · BOSTON

First published in 1992
by Faber and Faber Limited
3 Queen Square London WC1N 3AU

Photoset by Parker Typesetting Service, Leicester
Printed in Great Britain by
Cox and Wyman Ltd, Reading, Berkshire

A CIP record for this book is
available from the British Library
ISBN 0–571–16463–3

For my first grandchild
Isaac George Stroud Harwood
in the hope he likes
this sort of thing

CHARACTERS

SUSAN DAVIS
DEREK TEWBY
JAMES WILEY
REGINA MELNICK
ROBERT JAFFEY
ALFRED MANX
MICHAEL MANX

The play takes place in an old Thames warehouse which has been converted into a fringe theatre known as the Acropolis.

ACT ONE
9 pm on a Sunday in February

ACT TWO
Mid-morning, four weeks later

An old Thames warehouse has been converted into the Acropolis Theatre. It is not an ideal theatrical space but its architect has meant it to be flexible. And, of course, directors and designers who use the theatre have their own ideas: this is to be encouraged.

There are at least two doors. One leads to the foyer and to the street; another to the backstage area, dressing-rooms, a small rehearsal space, a green room.

In Act One, motifs of Van Gogh are evident because the stage area is set for the current production, a one-man show called *Theo* by Michael Manx with Derek Tewby as Theo van Gogh. There are also signs that the theatre, this evening, is being used for a party.

In Act Two, four weeks later, the stage is set for *Brother Mine*.

CAST

Reflected Glory was first presented by Mark Furness at the Civic Theatre, Darlington, on 19 February 1992, and subsequently at the Vaudeville Theatre, London on 8 April 1992, with the following cast:

SUSAN DAVIS	Holly Wilson
DEREK TEWBY	Nicky Henson
JAMES WILEY	Mark Tandy
REGINA MELNICK	Katherine O'Toole
ROBERT JAFFEY	Stephen Greif
ALFRED MANX	Albert Finney
MICHAEL MANX	Stephen Moore
Director	Elijah Moshinsky
Designer	Saul Rodomsky
Lighting	Paul Pyant
Sound	Ross Brown

ACT ONE

An evening in February, 9 pm. Very dark. Long silence. Then, out of the darkness, the sound of DEREK *spluttering with laughter. Whispers:*

SUSAN'S VOICE: Derek, ssh!

DEREK'S VOICE: Sorry, sorry –

SUSAN'S VOICE: Ssh, ssh!
    (*Silence.*)
    Jimmy, throw the switch the moment he opens the door –

JAMES'S VOICE: I know, I know, and when I've sung 'Happy Birthday' I bring up the rest of the lights –

SUSAN'S VOICE: We *all* sing, 'Happy Birthday'; we *all* sing 'Happy Birthday' –
    (*Whispers overlapping:*)

ROBERT'S VOICE: Yes, yes, we know –

JAMES'S VOICE: Of course we all sing 'Happy Birthday', I only said –

SUSAN'S VOICE: Ssh! Ssh! Stop shouting! Ssh!

REGINA'S VOICE: Susan, relax, for God's sake –

SUSAN'S VOICE: Ssh! Ssh!
    (*Silence. Sound of* DEREK *spluttering with laughter.*)
    Derek, please!

DEREK'S VOICE: Sorry, sorry, surprises make me nervous –
    (*He laughs nervously.*)

SUSAN'S VOICE: Ssh!
    (*Silence.*)

ROBERT'S VOICE: Susan, I honestly don't think there's anybody there –

SUSAN'S VOICE: Ssh!

REGINA'S VOICE: Michael's not due for another half-hour, better turn on the lights –

SUSAN'S VOICE: No, no, don't, he's here, I'm telling you, I heard him, Michael's here, ssh!
    (*A noise, then footsteps somewhere.*)

ROBERT'S VOICE: Ssh, ssh, there is someone –

I

SUSAN'S VOICE: Yes, yes, it's Michael, I told you, ssh!
THE OTHERS: Ssh! Ssh! Ssh! Ssh!
SUSAN'S VOICE: Ssh! Ssh!

>   (*Silence.*)
>   (*After a moment*) Ssh!
>   (*Silence again. A door opens. A light switch is thrown. Two spotlights, focused on the door, snap on, illuminating* ALFRED MANX. *He freezes like a rabbit caught in the light of a car. A collective gasp.*)

SUSAN: (*Horrified*) Alfred! What are you doing here?

>   (ALFRED MANX, *aged fifty-six, an impressive figure, is impeccably and expensively dressed in the very latest fashion. Caught in the light, he says nothing and is momentarily blinded. He steps forward and tries to adjust his eyes to the light. The others are:* SUSAN DAVIS, *forty-ish, nervy, attractive, sexily dressed;* REGINA MELNICK, *thirty-ish, handsome, calm, elegant;* JAMES WILEY, *thirty-ish, very handsome, wearing casual chic;* DEREK TEWBY, *thirty-ish, anonymous, ordinary, wearing sports jacket, flannels, tie;* ROBERT JAFFEY, *fifty-two, conventional, in a dark suit. All hold champagne glasses.* ALFRED *shields his eyes against the light.*)

ALFRED: (*Deeply suspicious*) Michael? Michael Manx, are you there?

SUSAN: (*Mounting hysteria*) Alfred, go away, you shouldn't be here, go away for God's sake!

ALFRED: (*Focusing on her*) Thank you, Susan, you always had the knack of making me feel welcome.

>   (JAMES *brings up more light.* SUSAN *is pacing this way and that.*)

SUSAN: Oh my God, oh my God, oh my God –

>   (ALFRED *adjusts to the lights.*)

ALFRED: Well, well. You're looking particularly lovely tonight, Susan, if a little strained. You've hardly changed. Where's our Michael?

SUSAN: Alfred, leave now. This instant. Immediately. This second. Now. Immediately. Now.

>   (ALFRED *ignores her and sees* ROBERT, *which surprises him.*)

ALFRED: Robert Jaffey! Fancy. It's nice to know my lawyer's

2

close at hand. I may want to sue somebody. What are you doing here, Robert? You've not become Michael's lawyer, too, have you?

ROBERT: (*Horribly embarrassed; vague gestures*) No, no, I'm – I – I – I was invited – I'm a guest of – I –

SUSAN: (*Cutting in*) Never mind Robert, what about *you*, Alfred, what are you doing here?

ALFRED: (*Smiling*) I was invited, too –

SUSAN: (*Shocked*) What do you mean, you were invited, too? Who invited you? Not me, it wasn't me –

ALFRED: Our Michael invited me –

SUSAN: (*Continuing, not taking it in at first*) – and no one else would have – what, who, what, who invited you?

ALFRED: Our Michael. Only he didn't tell me there'd be other people here. He's not changed either has our Michael, underhand, devious little runt, never tells the full story, am I right?

SUSAN: But this is a surprise party for him, he doesn't know anything about it, he couldn't possibly have invited you. It's his birthday –

ALFRED: It's Michael's birthday?

SUSAN: He's due any second, so just go now, we can talk about it tomorrow –

ALFRED: Of course! It's the *sixteenth*. Of course! Funny what you forget when you consign your own brother to outer darkness. Who else is here, then?

(DEREK *scuttles over to* SUSAN.)

DEREK: (Sotto voce, *with elaborate meaningless mime*) Is this the brother, is this – is this – is this – ?

SUSAN: (*Hissing*) Yes!

(DEREK *begins to watch* ALFRED, *almost as if hypnotized by him.*

ALFRED'S *eye lights on* JAMES, *whom he seems to recognize. He gives a half-smile of recognition.*)

ALFRED: I know you.

(JAMES *flicks a nervous smile back.* ALFRED *is fascinated by him, trying to work out who he is.* SUSAN *draws* REGINA *and* ROBERT *aside.*)

3

SUSAN: I've got to get hold of Michael. This is a disaster, what am I going to do, what am I going to do?

REGINA: Susan, calm down, there's nothing you can do, Michael's probably on his way by now –

(ALFRED's *attention is all on* JAMES .)

ALFRED: Excuse me for staring so rudely, but I know I know you very well indeed.

(JAMES *is about to speak*.)

No, no, whatever you do, don't tell me your name. I pride myself on remembering names. Wait a moment, wait a moment, I'll get it, I'll get it –

SUSAN: I have the most awful feeling Michael knows about the party –

REGINA: He can't know, and even if he did, why would he invite his brother?

SUSAN: I've no idea, but it's the sort of thing Michael gets up to –

ALFRED: Nobody's to tell me his name. Begins with F, am I right? No, no, don't tell me. Wait a moment, I'll get it, I'll get it – Fff –

(REGINA *and* SUSAN *continue confidentially*:)

REGINA: You know what I think? I think it's just an unfortunate coincidence, that's all –

ROBERT: I don't believe in coincidence.

REGINA: Well, they happen, dammit, they happen –

ALFRED: Fff – Fff – Fff –

ROBERT: I don't believe in them. I don't believe in accidents either. People engineer things of this kind, subconsciously, perhaps, but they engineer them. You may have let something slip –

REGINA: I didn't –

ALFRED: I know your name as well as I know my own, I know it, I know it, Fff – Fff – I used to watch you every week, what an actor you are, what an actor. My ex-wife, Jemima, she loved your smile. She used to say, 'That man's got the smile of the Venus de Milo.'

ROBERT: I have theories related to these matters in which I passionately believe. I believe all disasters, accidents, coincidences are subconsciously engineered –

4

REGINA: Robert, if you don't shut up I'll strangle you –

ALFRED: I can see your name now – Fff – Fff – Fff – I think I must have Alzheimer's – it's on the tip of my tongue –

ROBERT: Just because I'm a solicitor, Regina, doesn't mean I can't have theories.

SUSAN: (*Suddenly remembering*) Michael said he was going to see Billy. I'll telephone Billy – (*She rushes off.*)

ALFRED: It's coming! It's coming! Fff – Fff – Fff – (*He gives up.*) No, no, I'm sorry, I can't remember, you'll have to tell me. I'm very sorry. Tell me, please, what's your name?

JAMES: James Wiley.

ALFRED: You're right! You're absolutely right! James Wiley! You're right! Well I never! James Wiley!

DEREK: (*Quiet, amused*) Fff – Fff – Fff –

ALFRED: What an actor! Allow me to introduce myself. Alfred Manx. As you probably gathered, Michael Manx, the playwright and world-famous genius, is my brother, but we haven't seen each other for ten, eleven years. In fact, we haven't been on speaks for ten years.

JAMES: On speaks?

ALFRED: Not a word. Families. Brothers. What can I tell you? (*He takes out a small pack of business cards.*) I am the owner of the Café de la Poste, Church Road, Barnes, London, SW13, a restaurant that's not unknown, you follow me?

DEREK: (*Delighted*) You follow me!
(*Disconcerted,* ALFRED *stares at him.* REGINA *hurries to* DEREK *and has a quiet word.* ALFRED *returns his attention to* JAMES *and gives him a card.*)

ALFRED: Yes, a very good restaurant, even if I say so myself. In fact, I've been led to believe we can expect one knife and fork in the new *Guide Michelin*. James Wiley! Well, I never! My brother Michael knows them all, eh? I'm a bit of a performer myself, you follow me? When I was a kid I used to pretend to throw fits –
(*He twitches a bit, then laughs.* DEREK *makes a gesture of amazement, which* ALFRED *sees and tries to ignore.*)
Fooled two doctors with that. Oh yes, I was a performer, all right, always a bit of an actor, me. We used to learn

5

tap-dancing, Michael and me. And when we were kids –
(*He demonstrates a few steps of a soft-shoe shuffle, humming the tune 'Me and My Shadow'.* JAMES *and* DEREK *exchange a look.*)
– we brought the house down at the Christmas show of Miss Sybil Feinstein's Academy of Dance and Drama –
(*He beams; stops; gives a slight bow, now the restaurateur.*)
Mr Wiley, you're welcome any time at the Café de la Poste. In fact, you're all welcome any time –
(*He gives a card to* DEREK, *is about to give one to* ROBERT.)
No, you don't need one, Robert. Robert Jaffey's my solicitor, as you've also probably gathered, ladies and gentlemen, and Mr Jaffey has eaten at the Café de la Poste I can't count the times, and I've never let him pay the bill. But when I go to his office and see him – (*a pregnant look and smile*) – you follow me? The moment you walk in his door, on goes the meter – (*chuckles, looks round for approval*) – on goes the meter, you follow me? Like a taxi, tick-tick-tick-tick – don't worry, Robert, I'm only teasing, don't burst into tears, lawyers will be lawyers –

ROBERT: Alfred, I really think you ought to leave.

ALFRED: When I want your advice, Mr Jaffey, I'll pay for it. I'm not leaving so forget it.
(*He removes his overcoat, puts it over a chair.*)
I want to know what our Michael's up to, I want to know why I've been invited here with the rest of you. You see, I thought this was going to be a private meeting, just Michael and me, but then, of course, I'm a very private person, unlike Michael who's a very public figure, you follow me? He said he wanted a reconciliation. Well, you'd think a reconciliation, between two brothers, after all these years, was a private matter, am I right? Obviously not. No. Because with Michael nothing's private.
(*He approaches* REGINA *with a card.*)
How d'you do, you win the prize.

REGINA: Why? Because I'm the prettiest girl you've seen this week?
(*Smothered laughter from* JAMES *and* DEREK. ALFRED *is taken aback, thrown.*)

6

ALFRED: Have we met before?

REGINA: (*Amused*) No.

ALFRED: You're sure?

REGINA: Sure.

ALFRED: Fine, fine, because I don't know what you do for a living
but if you want to get into films, there's a big American
producer eats most evenings in my restaurant. Have dinner
with me, I'll introduce you, who knows where it'll lead?

REGINA: I'm Michael's agent.

ALFRED: His agent? Really? You look a bit young to be an agent.
You know you have to be over the age of consent to take
commission – (*chuckles, looks round for approval*) – over the age
of consent – commission –

DEREK: Amazing!

(ALFRED *is again a little disconcerted but only briefly.*)

ALFRED: All I can say is, you must be the most beautiful agent in
London. You're certainly better looking than Michael's first
agent whom I knew well, Norbert van Ryan, but that's not
difficult because he was bald with halitosis. (*Chuckles, looks for
approval.*) And your name, young lady, if I may be so bold?

REGINA: Regina Melnick.

ALFRED: (*Thunderstruck*) I beg your pardon!

REGINA: Regina Melnick.

(ALFRED *makes two or three short sounds that could be laughter or
grunts.*)

ALFRED: Hunh! hunh-hunh, hunh! Forgive me, please, Regina, if
I may be so familiar, forgive me for laughing, I am not
laughing at you, far from it, I never laugh at beauty, but – (*He
chuckles a lot now at the memory.*) We had a fellow in my class at
school, our Michael knew him, too, he was – I'm telling you
the absolute truth – he was – this big – (*mimes a ludicrously
short man*) – and his name was, yes, you've guessed it,
Melnick, Bernard Melnick. He was so small he could stand
under a table. On a box. Wearing a top hat. You know what
we used to call him? Listen to this, listen to this, we used to
call him – *Tiny* Melnick!

JAMES: You sound a very witty bunch.

ALFRED: We were, we were, Tiny Melnick, he could walk into this

7

room under a closed door. If you saw Michael's first play, *Family Matters*, you'll remember they talk about him. Tiny Melnick's the little fellow who liked to umpire the tennis tournament because when he sat in the umpire's chair it was the only way he could see the game. In the play Michael called him Shorty Trotter, but he was Tiny Melnick to a T. (*Chuckles at the memory.*) The last time I saw Tiny's name was in our old school magazine. He wrote an article about our Michael, the world-famous genius, but it never said what Tiny himself was up to. I often wonder what became of him. Tiny Melnick!

REGINA: He's a County Court Judge, he's my father.
(*No more than a flick from* ALFRED.)

ALFRED: Clever? A mind like a laser. Tiny was the cleverest boy in the school, in any school, in the whole of Manchester he was the cleverest boy. Top of the class. All subjects. The height must have gone to his brains, you follow me. Mind you, I'm not surprised he's a judge because he's still sitting up high looking down on a court.
(*He chuckles, looks round for approval, then is struck by a sudden memory.*)
Of course! I bet I know your mother. That's where you get your looks from. Because when Tiny was head prefect he was courting Zena Bernstein, my God, what a looker, and you know what we used to call her? We used to call her 'million-dollar legs'.

JAMES: I bet that was because she had nice legs.

ALFRED: James, if I may be so familiar, she had legs to make Cyd Charisse look like Hopalong Cassidy. (*To* REGINA.) Now, am I right, Zena Bernstein's your mother?

REGINA: No.

ALFRED: Well, there you are, there's no predicting the future. So, Regina, please do me the honour of bringing His Honour Judge Melnick to my restaurant. (*Genuine concern.*) Tell me, he didn't grow?
(*A stony stare from* REGINA.)
Never mind, we'll make him very comfortable. We've got lots of cushions –

8

DEREK: (*To* JAMES) Cushions –

(ALFRED *kisses her hand as* SUSAN *returns, near to tears, distraught.*)

SUSAN: I can't get hold of him, he's not at Billy's, he said he was going to Billy's but Billy says he never showed up, and now Alfred's here – I went to so much trouble – we all went to so much trouble – it's a disaster –

ALFRED: Think of it, Susan, as the *Titanic* meeting the iceberg. I'm the iceberg. You should know by now that Michael Manx, playwright, world-famous genius, *artiste extraordinaire*, your husband and my kid brother, is as devious as a Spanish wine-grower. (*He begins to look around.*) So, this is our Michael's theatre. This is the world-famous Acropolis Theatre. The Acropolis. Hunh. To me, it always sounds like a Greek taverna. I have scrupulously avoided coming to this place. I'll tell you what, it looks as though they ran out of money before they could finish it.

(*Now,* DEREK *surreptitiously and involuntarily begins to mimic* ALFRED, *trying to imitate his gestures, his walk, the angle of his head – like an annoying child.*)

Michael had a public appeal for this place, you know. I gave two hundred and fifty pounds. Anonymously. I'd like to know what they spent it on. I like a theatre to be a theatre, you follow me? Plush, that's what I like, plush. Velvet and regency stripes, that sort of thing. I have burgundy and cream striped wallpaper in the Café de la Poste punctuated with fleurs-de-lis in gold, the banquettes are covered in velvet and there are mirrors etched with naked maidens rising from the sea. A restaurant's theatre, you follow me, James? And a restaurateur has to be something of an actor. I mean, a restaurant does a crêpe Suzette, it's got to be dramatic. I always say, *flambé* is not *flambé* without flair. The customer wants to see the flames rise like the Leaning Tower of Pisa, am I right? Perhaps I should have been in the theatre because, like I said –

SUSAN: Alfred, when did Michael invite you?

(ALFRED *considers for a moment, then takes out a letter, looks at the date.*)

9

ALFRED: I received the invitation by letter last week.

SUSAN: Then he couldn't have known. I only decided to give the party two days ago.

(*General murmurs of agreement.*)

Alfred, there's been a ghastly mistake. Michael obviously invited you here for a private meeting. I didn't know he was doing that. In the meantime, I arranged a surprise birthday party for him. He didn't know I was doing that.

ALFRED: Doesn't say much for your marriage, does it?

(*He chuckles, looks round.*)

SUSAN: (*Trying to keep calm but failing*) Alfred, please listen to me. I want you to go. I don't know how to convince you that it's for the best, but, believe me, for everyone's sake, yours, Michael's, everyone's, it's better that you leave. You see, this is not only a birthday party, it's also to celebrate Michael's new play, 'Bro –'

(*The others tense.* ALFRED *looks from one to the other.* SUSAN *resumes.*)

His new play. We start rehearsals tomorrow. Michael's directing it, too. And so I thought – you see, Derek and James are in it, and so am I. I play – several parts – and, as you probably know, not many playwrights write good parts for women, and these are awfully good parts, and I haven't worked for some time, and if you stay here it may just ruin everything.

ALFRED: Don't give me that guff, please, Susan. I know your husband only too well. He's devious and totally devoid of any feeling. He wants a reconciliation with his brother to whom he hasn't talked for ten years and what does he do? He invites him to his own surprise party! Don't give me the guff. It's not me who's out to ruin everything. (*The short, sharp sounds again.*) Hunh! Hunh! Hunh-hunh! I know what Michael's up to. He wants an audience, he wants a public, that's all he knows, public, press, television, telling the world. Take it from me, if our Michael doesn't see his name in the paper of a morning, he thinks he's dead and stays in bed for the rest of the day. He hasn't changed. And Michael was always devious even as a baby. He'd never just cry to get attention, oh no, not our Michael. He'd get his head stuck in the bars of the playpen. And it had to be when the whole family was there. He never got his head stuck when he was alone, you follow me. Oh yes, likes an audience does our Michael. But, we must forgive him, mustn't we, because, well, because he's an artist, and artists are entitled to – are entitled to – hunh! Hunh-hunh! Cunning, secretive, devious. Listen to this, listen to this – (*Reading the letter.*) 'My dear Alfred, don't faint. Yes, it's your brother Michael writing this peace offering, so please read to the end. Dear, dear Alfred, a decade has passed since we talked face to face. Hasn't the time come when we should put our differences behind us? Hasn't the time come when, in memory of Mam and Dad, we should bury the ridiculous enmity that has savaged our relationship? I think often of our childhood, how close we were, and regret with all my heart that we ceased to be friends, that we ceased to be brothers. I regret the anger and the pain. I want a reconciliation. Please let's meet. I'd rather it wasn't at my home or at your restaurant. Let's meet on neutral ground. Could you be at my theatre, the Acropolis, next Sunday night, round about nine? Please, please be there. I'll explain everything when we meet. Dear, dear Alfred, we'll play tennis again – when my tennis elbow's better, that is. Your loving brother, Michael.' He's a beautiful writer, don't you think? But I'll tell you something, this letter is full of evasion and straightforward deviousness. He regrets but he doesn't apologize. But then, he's an Artist, am I right, Mr Jaffey? And you see, you see, he says 'neutral ground' but we're to meet in his theatre, and he doesn't say, 'It's my birthday', he doesn't say there'll be other people here, he doesn't –

SUSAN: He didn't know, he didn't know!

ALFRED: That's your story –

SUSAN: Oh God, you're such an unreasonable man –

ALFRED: I am not unreasonable, I just know my brother. He hasn't changed. No one changes. No one ever changes. Devious, underhand, crooked, cunning, secretive, that's how Michael is, that's how he's always been and I want to know what he's up to!

(SUSAN *bursts into tears and runs out.*)

(*Watching her go*) See? No one ever changes.

ROBERT: Should somebody go to her?

ALFRED: Leave her. She's happier crying. She always liked a good cry did Susan. When she married our Michael the tears she shed you'd think she was trying to sink Noah's Ark. She enjoys it, leave her be.

DEREK: I've noticed the characters in Michael's plays cry a lot.

ALFRED: That's because he's a bit of a crier himself is our Michael, but he was never in Susan's league. Our Michael's an emotional boy, you follow me, always was, always will be. Now, me? No, sir. I don't cry easily. An iceberg, me.

(DEREK *occasionally imitates him again behind his back – again involuntarily.*)

And he was always a hugger. I bet he's still a hugger. That got on my nerves. Always hugging and kissing, men, women, children, even complete strangers, I mean, after all, he's not a foreigner. No. No reserve, my brother Michael, no reserve. And, James, tell me, does he still have the habit of squeezing the back of your neck?

JAMES: Yes –

ALFRED: It always made me feel he was measuring me for the hangman's noose. Yes, funny boy, my brother, only he doesn't make me laugh. Art, Art was all he was interested in, you follow me? Art. My life is feeding the hungry, his life is Art. Art, fart, art, forgive me, Regina. Let me tell you, with Michael it has nothing to do with Art. With Michael fame is the spur, not Art. Money, prestige, position, power is the spur not Art. And if you're an artist, God forbid, one thing above all, you can forget your kith and kin. If you're an artist your kith and kin can go down the waste-disposer. I've got a few things to tell our Michael when I see him after all these years, don't you worry. Hunh! Hunh-hunh! Hunh!

(ROBERT *clears his throat, speaks very calmly and reasonably.*)

ROBERT: Alfred, you were one of my first clients and we've been through much together. So I feel entitled to talk to you not only as your legal adviser but also as your friend.

ALFRED: Have you turned the meter off?

(*He chuckles and looks round for approval.*)

ROBERT: I don't know what Michael's up to any more than you do. But, obviously, he wants to make his peace with you, he says as much in his letter, and for that, I think, we ought to take his word. Although, I admit, his exact motives for inviting you here tonight, on his birthday, with other guests, remain unclear. Whether he knows or not there is a surprise party is irrelevant. Now, I am not one to rehearse the past unnecessarily, but we went to litigation and we lost –

ALFRED: Yes, Mr Jaffey, we lost, and only because, with my luck, we had a bastard of a judge, a bastard literally, I'm not swearing, he was illegitimate, he'd been brought up in an orphanage so he hadn't got an ounce of family feeling. Now, if we'd had Tiny Melnick up there –

ROBERT: Alfred, let me finish. We lost our case. For whatever reasons. In the present circumstances, therefore, my advice to you is twofold. Either leave now or wait for Michael to arrive and see what he has to say. And if you choose the latter course, for heaven's sake, keep calm.

ALFRED: Keep calm, keep calm, is that your advice, Mr Jaffey? Are those the only words you can find to utter, keep calm? You know what I call advice like that? You know what I say when you talk like that, Mr Jaffey? I say you're talking Jaffenese! Keep calm? Keep calm? I have things to say to Michael, things that have been gnawing at my soul for ten years, longer, longer, eating into me like worms, and you say keep calm? Keep calm? Do you know the havoc he wrought on the whole Manx family? Do you know the misery, the shame, the embarrassment, the pain, he wrought on the whole Manx family? Hands up those of you who saw Michael's play, *Family Matters*.

(*Reluctantly, all hands eventually go up.*)

All right, you, Regina, what was the name of the family in that play?

REGINA: Marx.

ALFRED: Yes, Marx, good, ten out of ten. We're Manx, he calls them Marx. Michael turned the real Manx family into the Marx family for his play. That much he admitted in court. In the name of Art, he said. Mind you, I have to tell you, when my great-grandfather arrived here from Galicia his name *was* Marx but the immigration officer either mistook the 'r' for an 'n' so we became Manx, or, who knows, maybe he thought we came from the Isle of Man, it was never clear. All right. In the name of Art. 'An artist is entitled to use his own experience for his art.' Those are the exact words of the judge, the bastard, who had no family feeling and those words are engraved to this day on my heart. And, this may surprise you, I agree with the learned illegitimate judge. Wholeheartedly, you follow me? An artist is entitled to use his experience but! – not to *misuse* it. Keep calm? In the face of Michael telling the world our family secrets? Keep calm? In the face of those terrible lies he wrote, the distortions, the exaggerations, the cruelty? Keep calm? Hunh! Hunh-hunh! The lies, the lies and all in the name of Art! 'Writers are supposed to tell the truth, are supposed to be guardians of the truth' – my counsel's words in court, am I right, Mr Jaffey? – and Michael does nothing but distort and twist and make of us all a laughing-stock, yes, and all in the name of Art. How could he turn my poor old father into a drunk? My father, God rest his soul, a good man, a hardworking, responsible, sober man, whose same-day laundry service was the pride of Manchester, my father had one drink a year, a glass of sweet wine to make the blessing at Passover and then he'd pass out never mind pass over. And Michael turns him into an alcoholic who walks the streets at night in search of whores. And my mother, who slaved for us, encouraged and loved us, loved Michael more than any other human being in the world, he turned her into a shrew. All right, so after he was born she didn't want any more close contact with my father, and slept alone in another room, but to put that in a play for all the world to laugh at? And all in the name of Art? These are family secrets, private, sacred, family secrets. No, no, no, I cannot keep calm. I don't approve of lies. And most of all I hate cruelty. What Michael did was unforgivably cruel. Why, I ask, why in this world of sorrow, why cause unnecessary pain? And if that foundling who became a judge had one ounce of family in his veins he would have granted the injunction. But Michael was too clever. He left me out of the play. He made himself, the so-called hero, an only child. In the name of Art? No, in the name of playing safe! But you think I didn't recognize myself in that other play he wrote for the telly, *The Chef*? You remember the one, the bloke who could only cook one dish, an *entrecôte Bercy*? Won all sorts of prizes, that play did. For weeks afterwards customers came into the restaurant asking for *entrecôte Bercy* and I've never had it on my menu, never. And I'll tell you something, James, the actor who played the chef, the way he chopped onions you'd have found the tops of his fingers in the sauce, you follow me. It was totally inaccurate in every way. I wanted to have another go at Michael over that play, but Mr Jaffey here prevented me. I tell you for free if I'd have got him into court he'd even now be doing time in Strangeways.

(*He turns suddenly on* DEREK.)

Are you making fun of me? You've been making fun of me ever since I arrived. What's so funny? Are you getting pleasure out of mocking me? Don't you know it's very rude to mock people?

DEREK: I'm sorry, I'm sorry, I'm terribly sorry, I can explain –

REGINA: (*Stepping in quickly*) No, you can't.

(*A brief silence.*)

ALFRED: I apologize for flaring up like that. I have a bit of a temper, you follow me. I live alone and therefore don't have much opportunity for intelligent conversation. I'm sorry. Certain things trouble me profoundly. Certain things I feel deeply, and I'm troubled. I have a very short fuse.

(*Recovering his bonhomie*) You won't find a good restaurateur with a long fuse, you follow me? I'm sorry. I'm really very sorry.

(*Awkward silence.*)

JAMES: Funny you should talk about crying like that. I remember when I was playing Vershinin in *The Three Sisters* –

DEREK: I didn't know you'd played Vershinin, where was that?

JAMES: Edinburgh.

DEREK: Oh, Edinburgh, right. Who directed?

15

JAMES: That's the point, Tony Thompson –

DEREK: Oh my God.

JAMES: I know, what a wanker. He wanted me to cry all the time. And I said, 'Tony, dear, it's not the character, it's not Vershinin, it's not me', and d'you know what he said, he said, 'Just do as you're told, ducky.' I mean, to me, just do as you're told! And then I found this letter Chekhov had written complaining about Stanislavsky. 'Why do they all cry so much? Why does he make them all cry so much?' Chekhov said. So, of course, I showed the letter to Tony, and do you know what he said, he said, 'Yes, well, Chekhov's dead now, isn't he?' Prick.

DEREK: They're all wankers, darling. I had exactly the same problem with Harvey White, I was playing Rosencrantz –

JAMES: Whose Hamlet?

DEREK: Bob Fraser –

JAMES: (*Wincing*) You poor sod.

DEREK: Well, you know what they said, don't you? They said he was the best Hamlet since Sarah Bernhardt.

(JAMES *laughs*.)

And, wait for this, it was uncut! Four bloody hours of bloody *Hamlet* with Bob bloody Fraser. Anyway, Harvey White, our fearless leader, wanted me to run down left at some point, *run* down left, for no rhyme or reason, except that it suited his design concept –

JAMES: Oh yes, design concept, a synonym for sod the actors –

DEREK: Precisely, so I said, 'Mr White, excuse me.' I was very polite, as you know I've never been known to cause a fuss, I never lose my temper, I said, 'Mr White,' I said, 'why do I run at this point, I can't think of any reason why Rosencrantz should *run*, can you?' And he said, 'Just do it, I'll buy you a beer.'

JAMES: They're all the same –

ALFRED: (*To* ROBERT) Do you feel excluded? I feel excluded. It's funny how theoreticals can make ordinary people feel excluded. That's what my late father, God rest his soul, used to call theatricals. Theoreticals. (*To* DEREK.) I didn't take it in that you were also a theoretical. Because, I'll tell you what,

16

you don't look like a theoretical to me, you don't look like an
actor.

DEREK: How should an actor look?

ALFRED: (*Jerking a thumb at* JAMES) Like him.

DEREK: (*Cheerful*) We can't all be leading men, can we?

ALFRED: (*A sudden revelation*) Wait a moment, I've got you! Of
course! 'Fifteen men on a dead man's chest!' You're the
pirate in the Planter's Rum commercial, am I right?

DEREK: Yes –

ALFRED: Of course, I didn't recognize you without your crutch!
Do the accent, do the accent, I love the accent –

DEREK: No, no –

JAMES: Yes, go on, you're marvellous at it –

DEREK: No, no, no –

ROBERT: Oh, please do –

DEREK: No, really, under no circumstances, I simply will not –

ALFRED: Go on, go on –

DEREK: No! I will not!

REGINA: Please –

DEREK: (à la *Robert Newton as Long John Silver*) 'Well, my
hearties, top o' the mornin' to you, time's come for a little
light refreshment. Break open the stores, Jim-lad.'
(*Sings*) 'Fifteen men on a dead man's chest,
    Yo-ho-ho and a Planter's Rum!'

ALFRED: (*Applauding*) Bravo! Bravo!

DEREK: As a matter of fact, it's been frightfully lucrative for me
that commercial. Keeps me going very nicely, thank you
ever so much. And voice-overs, of course. That's how I can
afford to work here at the Acropolis. Michael pays absolutely
nothing, as I don't have to tell you. You see, I'm doing two
plays on the trot for Michael. I'm starring here at the
moment. Michael's put together a little one-man show for me
about Theo van Gogh –

ALFRED: *Theo* van Gogh? Who's he, if I may show my ignorance?

DEREK: You see? I said *Theo* was a bad title, we should have
called it *Vincent*. Theo van Gogh was Vincent van Gogh's
brother and it's really very touching because I was the only
person in the whole world who believed in Vincent's genius.

I was the only person to whom he could turn and, well, I loved him. Like a brother.

ALFRED: Michael seems to have brothers much on his mind just at the moment.

DEREK: Yes, and one-man shows are all the rage these days. We're playing to capacity. And the funny thing was, the play had rotten reviews, they said it was sentimental, lightweight, avoids the issues. Don't mention drama critics to Michael whatever you do. But I came off rather well. They were awfully kind to me. And in the next play –

REGINA: (*Cutting in sharply*) I thought Bob Fraser was a wonderful Hamlet –

JAMES: Oh did you?

REGINA: At least he was wonderful in parts –

JAMES: Sweetheart, if you can't be wonderful in parts of *Hamlet* you should give up the profession. Did you see his Shylock? I thought he played it like a Jewish lesbian.

ROBERT: (*Dry*) If there is such a thing.

(SUSAN *returns*.)

SUSAN: I think we should all go. I think we should leave Alfred here to wait for Michael.

REGINA: Good idea. We'll all go now and leave the brothers to it.

ALFRED: This is like one of his plays, you never know what's going on until the end and even then you don't know. But I'll tell you something for nothing. Alone or in company, he'll rue the day he asked for a reconciliation. I'll tell him one or two things that'll give him sleepless nights for the rest of his life. When I think of the pain –

REGINA: (*Interrupting*) Why don't we all come back and eat at our place? Fetch the food and some drink. Robert, get the chocolate mousses –

ROBERT: (*Hissed*) I'm not speaking to you –

REGINA: What have I done now?

ROBERT: The way you talk to me in public is disgraceful –

REGINA: Oh, don't be so pompous.

ROBERT: I'm not speaking to you –

ALFRED: You two sound very lovey-dovey – (*Chuckles, looks round for approval.*) Lovey-dovey –

(MICHAEL *enters.*)

MICHAEL: (*Shocked*) What's going on?

    (*They all swing round.*)

REGINA: Michael!

    (MICHAEL MANX, *fifty-one, is sometimes ingratiating and over-friendly. He has a crooked, faraway smile and a laugh that sounds like a hiss. He is untidy and his clothes are 'studied scruff'.* DEREK *starts to sing 'Happy Birthday' but after a few bars loses confidence and stops.* MICHAEL *and* ALFRED *stare at each other in thunderous silence. Then:*)

ALFRED: Michael Manx, after ten years of silence and separation I have some things to say to you –

    (*He falls silent. The brothers gaze at each other. The others watch nervously. When the tension is unbearable,* ALFRED *bursts into tears.*)

    Michael, Michael, Michael –

    (MICHAEL *bursts into tears.*)

MICHAEL: Alfie, oh, Alfie –

    (*They fall into each other's arms, weeping profusely, hugging each other tightly.* SUSAN *cries.* REGINA *cries.* ROBERT *takes a handkerchief and wipes tears from his eyes. The crying continues.*)

JAMES: (*To* DEREK) I think I may vomit.

    (ALFRED *takes* MICHAEL'*s face in his hands and gazes into his eyes.*)

ALFRED: Micky, Michael, Mick, Mick, Mick –

    (*They hug. Between hugs and tears* ALFRED *manages to speak.*) I had things – things to say to you – they've gone from my mind – just seeing you again – it's been too long – brother mine –

    (*A startled reaction from the others, which* ALFRED *doesn't notice.*)

    – my knees have turned to aspic – I can't remember a word of what I wanted to say – all I know is – I've got this picture in my head of Mam and Dad up there, God rest their souls, looking down on us together again, and they're smiling, Micky, they're smiling –

    (ALFRED *breaks from the embrace, turns away, weeps like a baby.* MICHAEL *tries to comfort him.* ALFRED *starts to retch.*)

The toilet –

(MICHAEL *points to a door.* ALFRED *rushes off.* MICHAEL *turns to the others.*)

MICHAEL: (*Bewildered; the crooked smile*) I don't understand this, what are you all doing here?

SUSAN: It's a surprise party, sweetheart.

MICHAEL: For whom?

SUSAN: For you.

MICHAEL: A surprise party? Why didn't you tell me?

(*No response.*)

SUSAN: (*Tearful*) I suppose you want us all to go –

MICHAEL: (*Wiping away tears*) No, no, no, no. I want you all to stay. This is so lovely. Just by the way, did anyone mention the new play to him?

REGINA: (*Wiping away tears*) No, no, it was touch and go once or twice but I managed –

MICHAEL: Good, good, because we have to be so careful with him, so careful. We're on such dangerous ground. (*To* SUSAN.) A surprise party. You sweetheart –

SUSAN: Have you taken your tablets?

(*He nods. They kiss. He goes to* ROBERT *and embraces him.* ROBERT *remains rigid.*)

MICHAEL: You can't imagine how important this night is to me, old darling. I haven't seen Alfred for – for ten years – we haven't spoken – for – for ten years –

ROBERT: (*Recovered; dry*) We know.

(MICHAEL *embraces* JAMES *and* DEREK *together.*)

MICHAEL: Boys, boys, I'm so upset, I can hardly articulate, I didn't imagine I'd be so upset seeing him again –

(REGINA *meanwhile, has produced a small package.*)

REGINA: Happy birthday, Michael darling. From Robert and me.

MICHAEL: Oh, Regina, for me? Thank you.

(*He tears open the package: a gold pen.*)

(*Trying to cheer up.*) A pen. That's my agent, folks. Gives me a pen. Wants me to keep at it!

(*Mild laughter.*)

Thanks, Robert. Thanks, Reggie. What would I do without you?

20

(DEREK *and* JAMES *approach with packages, which they give
to* MICHAEL *who starts to open them.*)

JAMES: Happy birthday.

DEREK: Yes, happy birthday.

MICHAEL: Oh, boys, you shouldn't, you shouldn't –

DEREK: Just something small. Although I always say it's not the
thought that counts, it's the gift.

(ALFRED *returns, wiping his face with a handkerchief.*
MICHAEL *holds up shaving foam and aftershave.*)

MICHAEL: Givenchy. I must be overpaying you. (*He laughs as
though hissing.*) Thanks, boys.

(*He squeezes the backs of their necks.*)

SUSAN: My present was the surprise party.

MICHAEL: Sweetheart.

(*He embraces and kisses her.*)

ALFRED: I came empty-handed. I simply didn't put two and two
together, February sixteenth, I should have remembered –

MICHAEL: Alfred, just you being here is the best present I've
ever had. No offence to anyone else, these are lovely gifts,
but I'm sure you all understand. Alfie and I –

(*He looks lovingly at* ALFRED.)

ROBERT: Do the brothers want to be private?

THE OTHERS: (*Over-enthusiastic*) Yes, yes, what a good idea,
leave them to it, yes, yes, what a good idea –

SUSAN: Why doesn't everyone come and eat, there's heaps of
food –

(*They are gone in a flash leaving* MICHAEL *and* ALFRED *alone.
Silence.*)

ALFRED: I've just been sick.

MICHAEL: Alfie.

ALFRED: I came here tonight full of bile and anger. I came with
murder in my heart.

MICHAEL: I know, I know –

ALFRED: And it seemed to vanish in a flash. I saw you and I
regurgitated.

MICHAEL: Perhaps you'd like to rephrase that.

(ALFRED *smiles.* MICHAEL *hisses.*)

I should have written to you years ago.

21

ALFRED: I had things in my mind, things I've been rehearsing to say to you, and they've all gone –

MICHAEL: I'm pleased, I'm really pleased. Gee, Alfie, this is nice –

ALFRED: I used to write you letters, terrible, terrible letters, then I'd tear them up, then I'd start again, tear them up, start again, tear them up. I'd talk aloud as if you were there, you follow me, say such things you wouldn't believe. But when I saw you tonight, looking just the same, it was like a burden lifting, like – (*smiles*) – like a – souffle rising.

MICHAEL: I know I've caused you terrible unhappiness, Alf, but the past is the past, right, Alfie?

ALFRED: Right, Right. The past is the past.

(*Silence.*)

MICHAEL: You've been well?

ALFRED: Mustn't grumble. And you? How have you been?

MICHAEL: I had ingrowing toenails on my big toes. Both of them. Agony, you can't imagine. And a rash on my face. That broke out the day after I wrote to you. My skin specialist said it was psychosomatic. And I've got terrible tennis elbow at the moment. I can hardly grip anything –

ALFRED: I'm sorry I asked –

MICHAEL: You know me, Alf, I have bouts of good health.

ALFRED: And the ulcers? You still have the ulcers?

MICHAEL: They aren't ulcers. I had tests, Alfie, you wouldn't believe. Ever had a barium meal?

(ALFRED *shakes his head.*)

You're lucky. *Haute cuisine* it is not.

ALFRED: So what's the matter with you?

MICHAEL: Gastritis. Nervous stomach. I have to eat a little, but often. I have tablets. They taste of chalk. Terrible.

(*He smiles his crooked, martyred smile.*)

ALFRED: I read about you all the time, Mick. It's difficult not picking up a paper without seeing your name. I hope you're happy. Apart from your aches and pains and nervous stomach, I hope you've realized your ambitions. I –

MICHAEL: And you, Alfie?

ALFRED: Me? I have a wonderful life. Up at five every morning,

22

off to market, see all my old mates, the butcher, the baker, the candlestick maker. 'Hello, Alf,' they say and I know them all by their first names. It's like a family, you follow me. Same at the restaurant. I'm hard on the staff. I won't stand for second best. But they don't hold that against me. I'm a professional. I admire professionals. Some of them have been with me ten years, more. I suppose they laugh at me behind my back but – they're family, too. And the customers, the regulars, we all know each other, laugh, joke, chat. I love it. I wake up each day – (*Lost for a moment.*) No, I don't really know them, Mick. And they don't really know me. We don't really talk, you follow me. It's all façade, am I right? I hope you're happy, Mick.

MICHAEL: Happy, happy, I don't set store by happiness, Alf. I do what I do. I am what I am. How're the twins?

ALFRED: Lovely. They're two lovely boys, thank God, touch wood.

MICHAEL: What are they up to?

ALFRED: Brent's in Zurich doing hotel management and Perry is studying to be an accountant.

MICHAEL: Wonderful, wonderful. You know something, Alfie? I've often dreamed we'd come together again. I've often thought we'd go back home, see the old places, chew the fat, jaw about times past, take the bus into Piccadilly –

ALFRED: Chat up the girls –

MICHAEL: Down these mean streets a man must go!

ALFRED: (*Calling softly*) Ariadne! Ariadne!

MICHAEL: (*Inexplicably uncomfortable*) You remember Ariadne?

ALFRED: How could I forget Ariadne? And the tennis. Did you ever get a set off me?

MICHAEL: When my elbow's better, we'll play again.

ALFRED: And, Michael, Michael, you remember when I used to get so angry I couldn't speak, I used to pin you down and lick your face?

MICHAEL: (*Taken aback*) What?

ALFRED: How I used to lick your face, do you remember?

MICHAEL: Do I remember?

ALFRED: That's what's I'm asking, do you remember?

MICHAEL: 'Course I remember how you licked my face –

ALFRED: (*Softly*) 'Me and my shadow – '

(MICHAEL *moves away*.)

And you remember Miss Sybil Feinstein's Academy of Dance and Drama? I was telling them earlier – do her voice, Mick, do her voice –

(*A brief pause*.)

MICHAEL: (*Imitating a female voice*) 'What are those at the end of your legs, Alfred? Oh, I see, they're your feet!'

(*They laugh,* ALFRED *rather more than* MICHAEL *whose hiss comes in short bursts. Awkward silence*.)

ALFRED: I'm going to confess something to you. Often, I'm introduced as your brother. 'This is Michael Manx's brother,' people say. And if they don't introduce me as your brother, I somehow manage to get it in. 'I'm Michael Manx's brother,' I say. There's a kind of glory in it for me. In fact, if I were to tell the truth, I'm proud of being Michael Manx's brother.

(*Awkward silence*.)

MICHAEL: You never married again.

ALFRED: No. Jemima was the first and last. And I should never have married her, Mick.

MICHAEL: You remember Dad being taken ill at the reception?

ALFRED: What reception?

MICHAEL: Your wedding reception.

ALFRED: Dad taken ill at my wedding reception? What are you talking about? He was taken ill later, much later –

MICHAEL: Was he? I could have sworn – (*Abrupt change of tack*.) I heard you were living with someone.

ALFRED: Yeah, Veronica, her name was. Eleven months it lasted, that's all. Eleven months.

MICHAEL: I'm sorry, I hope it wasn't too painful. I was told she was a good influence.

ALFRED: A good influence, my eye. She was good under the influence, more like.

(*Awkward silence*.)

MICHAEL: Alfie –

ALFRED: What?

MICHAEL: I have a surprise for you. (*Hesitates.*) I've – I've
dedicated my new play to you. It's a peace offering.

ALFRED: Oh, Mick, that's nice. That's really nice. What's it
called? Got a good catchy title?

(MICHAEL *paces, hands in pocket.*)

MICHAEL: I think it's a good play. Change of style for me.
Episodic, not straight narrative –

ALFRED: You still do that –

MICHAEL: Do what?

ALFRED: Walk with your hands in your pockets. I always
remember our Mam saying, 'Michael, don't do that.
Confucius he say, "Man who walk down street with hands in
pocket feels cocky."'

(*They both laugh with pleasure.*)

So, tell me about the play.

(MICHAEL *paces again.*)

MICHAEL: Everybody who's read it thinks it's more than all right.
Regina Melnick, my agent, who can be pretty hard on me,
she's particularly pleased. It's going to be done all over the
place, there's already talk of a New York –

ALFRED: Here, did you know your agent's Tiny Melnick's
daughter? Did you know he's a judge now?

MICHAEL: Of course I know. We met at one of the school
reunions. He introduced me to Regina. We had dinner with
him only last week.

ALFRED: You had dinner with Tiny? How is he?

MICHAEL: Tiny.

ALFRED: Was he talking to you?

MICHAEL: Of course he was talking to me. We had dinner
together. Why shouldn't he be talking to me?

ALFRED: Shorty Trotter, the umpire's chair, in the play, in the
play –

MICHAEL: He didn't recognize himself.

ALFRED: He didn't recognize himself? How could he miss? Three
foot six, climbing up to the umpire's chair, it was what he
used to do, it was him to the life.

MICHAEL: He didn't recognize himself, what can I tell you. Most
people don't.

ALFRED: Unbelievable. Here, Mick, I fancy his daughter. Rotten. But I think Robert Jaffey's giving her one, am I right?

MICHAEL: They've been living together for two years.

ALFRED: There's no accounting for taste. She'd be better off with a mashed banana. I really fancy her, Mick.

MICHAEL: You won't get anywhere.

ALFRED: Why, have you tried?

MICHAEL: No, you know me, but they call her 'Tin-knickers'.

ALFRED: I'll make a bet with you. This time next week she'll be having dinner with me by candlelight.

MICHAEL: You're wasting your time, Alf.

ALFRED: Name the stakes.

MICHAEL: A tenner.

ALFRED: Done.

(*They shake hands.*)

MICHAEL: Done.

(*Uneasy pause.* ALFRED *holds on to* MICHAEL's *hand.*)

ALFRED: What's the new play about, Michael, what's it called, the one you've dedicated to me?

MICHAEL: Alfie, I'm going to make amends.

ALFRED: That's a long title, but I like it.

(*He chuckles.* MICHAEL *hisses.* SUSAN *enters with a vacuum flask and a packet of arrowroot biscuits.*)

SUSAN: Here's your supper, sweetheart.

ALFRED: Go on, what's the new play about, Mick?

SUSAN: You haven't been upsetting him, have you, Alfred? He musn't be upset. And you'd better come and eat. There won't be anything left. There are actors in there, you know. (*She goes.*)

MICHAEL: Go and eat. And afterwards, I'll tell you all about it. (MICHAEL *sits, pours himself milk from the vacuum flask, nibbles a biscuit.*)

ALFRED: (*He starts to go, stops.*) I can't get over Tiny Melnick not recognizing himself.

(*He goes.* MICHAEL *holds on to his head as if he's trying to keep it in place.* DEREK *with a plate of food, re-enters.*)

DEREK: Is this a good time to have a word?

MICHAEL: Not really, lovey, do you mind?

DEREK: You know the long bit in Act Two, describing Vincent's life in Arles, I'm getting laughs and I don't know why –

MICHAEL: Not now, Derek, there's a darling –

(JAMES *and* ROBERT *wander in with food.*)

DEREK: Will you come and see it this week? It's damned lonely doing a one-man show, you can't discuss it with anybody, there's no one to talk to, I mean, you're entirely on your own.

MICHAEL: Of course, it's a one-man show. Try being a playwright, old darling.

DEREK: Have you told your brother?

MICHAEL: Almost.

DEREK: I must say he's absolutely fascinating. The swings of mood, the anger, the speech patterns, the mannerisms. The little bits of pain flying about –

MICHAEL: Derek, excuse me, will you, I have to think something through. Don't worry. You're lovely as Theo. Everybody's singing your praises. I'll come and see the show at the end of the week. Oh, and don't discuss the new play with Alfred, will you? It's important you don't. I want to be the one to tell him.

(*He squeezes the back of* DEREK's *neck and goes.*)

DEREK: I know what Alfred means about the hangman's noose.

(REGINA *enters with puddings.*)

REGINA: Ready for pud?

(ROBERT *rises and draws her aside.*)

ROBERT: Has Michael told him?

REGINA: I thought you weren't speaking to me.

ROBERT: This is the worst party I've ever been to.

(*He goes, comes back to her, takes a pudding and moves aside as* ALFRED *enters.*)

ALFRED: (*To* REGINA) I believe you have the dessert.

REGINA: I'm sorry, I didn't realize –

(*He takes one and eats it at amazing speed. He smacks his lips as if checking the taste.*)

ALFRED: Who catered this function?

JAMES: I beg your pardon?

ALFRED: All my problems are solved.

ROBERT: What are you talking about now, Alfred?

ALFRED: I'm talking about this dessert, this delicacy, this chocolate mousse. Who catered this function?

REGINA: We all did a course. Derek did the *coq au vin*, James did the vegetables and I made the chocolate mousse.

ALFRED: You made this? You made this glorious chocolate mousse?

REGINA: Don't go overboard, it's nothing really, just whipped cream and –

ALFRED: Nothing, she says, nothing, you hear this woman, she says nothing? I am tasting the nectar of the gods and she says nothing. You ought to be ashamed of yourself. I have been looking for a dessert chef for the Café de la Poste for several weeks now. I've tried Swiss, Austrian, French, and not one of them came near to matching this creation. This is a mousse of talent and, believe me, I know what I'm talking about. Regina, I'm going to ask you to give me the recipe. Because I'm going to serve it in the restaurant and I'm going to call it Chocolate Mousse Regina Melnick, and I'm going to ask you to have dinner with me the first night it's on the menu. Next week.

REGINA: It's just from a cookery book, as a matter of fact I thought it was too sweet –

ALFRED: Too sweet? She has made a chocolate mousse to rank with the Taj Mahal and she says too sweet. Will you have dinner with me next week at the Café de la Poste the first night it's on the menu?

REGINA: You can't be serious –

ALFRED: About catering I'm always serious. Please. Next week. Chocolate Mousse Regina Melnick.

REGINA: (*Moving away*) Don't be ridiculous –

(*He is about to follow her when* DEREK *tugs him by the sleeve.*)

DEREK: Didn't you like my *coq au vin*?

ALFRED: I liked it. Oh yes, it was not without interest. But let me give you some advice. With *coq au vin*, you not only need good *coq* you also need good *vin*. And if I'm not mistaken, you used frozen *coq*, from a supermarket and *vin* that comes

28

in a bottle with a plastic top. Also you used Spanish onions, chopped. With *coq au vin* little French onions are essential. And never, never tinned mushrooms. I'm sorry to be harsh, but, in cooking, as in all things, the quality of the ingredients is all that matters, you follow me. You can serve cow dung off silver platters but it's still cow dung. I expect it's the same in the theatre.

DEREK: I'm sorry.

ALFRED: Don't be down-hearted. You'd probably say the same if you saw me as Rosencrantz. Excuse me –

(*He goes to* REGINA.)

Regina, I'm serious. This chocolate mousse has an after-taste better than Château-Lafite. Next Wednesday, eight o'clock, the Café de la Poste, Chocolate Mousse Regina Melnick, in the presence of the creator.

REGINA: Thank you, but I don't think so –

ALFRED: I'm conveying upon you immortality and you're turning me down. I'm putting you on a menu with Arnold Bennett, Nellie Melba and Bloody Mary.

(*She laughs quietly.*)

I must warn you if you don't come I shall bombard you with telephone calls, letters, flowers, poetry, maybe even copies of the menu and my menus are pure poetry. I can be very persistent. Come on, what's to lose? We'll have some fun.

ROBERT: Am I invited, too?

ALFRED: No, Robert, you're not.

REGINA: (*Smiling; to* ALFRED) All right. It's a date.

ALFRED: Excuse me, I have something to tell Michael –

(*He goes. Awkward silence. After a moment:*)

ROBERT: Did you like Edinburgh?

JAMES: Edinburgh?

ROBERT: I've always thought it a very attractive city. Edinburgh. The Paris of the North.

JAMES: Well, I only had one play out. It was a monstrous season as far as I was concerned. Mind you, I had a lovely run of parts. Vershinin in *Three Sisters*, Charles in *School for Scandal* and Elyot in *Private Lives*. We were going to bring *Private Lives* into London but we couldn't find a theatre. It's all musicals nowadays, you see, all the London theatres want musicals. Of course, I can sing. And I dance a little, I'm no Fred Astaire, but I get by. As a matter of fact, Derek and I have to do a bit of a song and dance in Michael's new play. That's why when Alfred mentioned it –

(*Sings.* DEREK *joins in:*)

   'Me and my shadow,

   Walking down the avenue – '

(*In the middle of song and dance* ALFRED *rushes in.*)

ALFRED: Who's singing that?

JAMES and DEREK: Me.

ALFRED: I don't believe it – (*Calling.*) Michael! Michael! Here a moment, this is amazing, Michael!

   (MICHAEL *returns, followed by* SUSAN.) You'll never guess what James Wiley was just singing?

MICHAEL: What?

   (ALFRED *goes into 'Me and My Shadow'.*)

ALFRED: Come on, Mick, let's show them how it's done –

MICHAEL: I can't, Alf, my elbow –

ALFRED: What do you mean? You're not going to dance on your elbow. Come on, do your best, it's a party and what a party! Good old Sybil Feinstein!

   (*He sings and dances.* MICHAEL *somewhat reluctantly joins in behind him as the 'shadow'. The others enjoy it. While they dance:*)

Come on, admit it, we've got style.

   (*Then:*)

I was always better than him.

   (*Then, to* MICHAEL:)

I can't remember when I was last so happy.

   (MICHAEL *suddenly breaks off.*)

MICHAEL: Alf, the play's called *Brother Mine*.

ALFRED: (*Offguard*) What –?

   (*Sudden stillness.* MICHAEL *smiles, He puts his arm through* ALFRED's, *walks him about.*)

MICHAEL: Yes, Alf, the new play, the one I've dedicated to you, it's called *Brother Mine*. It's about you, Alf, about us, about Jemima, oh Alf, you'll love it, it's got everything, 'Me and

My Shadow', tennis, Ariadne. And, everyone here's
involved, well, not Robert of course, but Derek and Jimmy,
they play us, Susan plays all the women, she's going to be
terrific as Ariadne and it's so wonderful you being here
tonight, one of us. Don't you feel part of a mighty enterprise,
Alfie? You're one of us. We're in it together, brother mine. 'I
see you stand like greyhounds in the slips,/Straining upon
the start!' And it's dedicated to you, Alf. As soon as it's
printed I'm going to present you with a leather-bound copy.
The dedication reads, 'To my brother, Alfred Manx, this
token of reconciliation, in gratitude and love.'

ALFRED: (*Terrible disappointment*) Oh, Michael, what do you
want to go and do a thing like that for? Can't you find
something else to write about? Why does it always have to be
Mam and Dad and me –?

MICHAEL: Mam and Dad don't come into it, I promise you, oh,
well, you hear Mam's voice, and a bit about Dad's will, but
nothing else, nothing to offend, I promise you. Alfie, you're
going to be so proud. I've made you the hero, Alf. Haven't I?

SUSAN *and* JAMES: Yes, absolutely –

DEREK: A saint –

MICHAEL: You'll be immortal –

(*Silence.*)

ALFRED: (*Quiet, inward*) Why do you do it, Mick? Why do you
want to crucify your own family?

MICHAEL: Alfie, Alfie, what are you talking about, crucifixion?
It's a celebration, Alf, of you and me. It's my way of making
amends. I want to be friends with you again, I want us to be
brothers again, for Mam and Dad's sake, God rest their
souls –

(*A brief pause.*)

ALFRED: You'd better let me read it.

MICHAEL: I don't want you to read it, Alf, plays aren't written to
be read, they're difficult to read. And we'll be making
changes all through rehearsals, cutting and adding lines,
maybe whole scenes, just come and see it, Alf –

ALFRED: You're making me nervous, Michael, you're making me
suspicious, you're making me anxious –

31

MICHAEL: Alfie, relax, don't get excited, I swear there's nothing in the play that'll upset you –

ALFRED: I want to be the judge of that –

(MICHAEL *paces, stops, turns.*)

MICHAEL: Alfie, let me try and explain, let me plead my case. I'm going to come clean, Alfie. (*He smiles crookedly.*) You see, Alf, I'm plagued by certain events, repetitive, tedious, powerful events. At least, they're powerful to me, that's the point. Powerful to me. I'm plagued by them, Alfie. It's because my roots are central to me. To my work. This is true of a great many artists. And these roots, these events, all from childhood or adolescence or early manhood – I don't know why but they stop in early manhood – these events and experiences dictate to my imagination and, I'm not exaggerating, they enslave me. Alfie. And, because I'm a writer, I'm compelled to write them down. And – and – and I have to try to give these events shape, point, counterpoint, to discern patterns, to try to find meaning, so that I can be free of them, Alf. Because I write only about events which are unresolved. And our relationship is, was, to say the least, unresolved. (*He paces, hands in pockets.*) This bad blood between us, Alfie –

SUSAN: Sit down, sweetheart, don't get tense.

MICHAEL: What?

SUSAN: Sit down, you're pacing –

MICHAEL: (*Venomous*) I'm all right, Susan! Shit, what was I saying? Yes, yes, our row, our argument, our separation all over one of my plays, it's been like a – like a tyrant seizing power, annexing my brain, holding it captive. I try to escape but I can't. Day and night, sleeping or waking, it's like having a prison guard with a gun trained on me. I've tried to write about it countless times but it abhorts and comes to nothing. It won't leave me alone. I just have to find out how and why we built up such hatred between us. Not hatred but, but enmity. I woke one night not long ago burning with an idea of how to write about it. I went to my desk and worked for four, five days with hardly any sleep, hardly any food –

32

SUSAN: And every time I interrupted with his milk and biscuits he bit my head off, but the doctor said –

MICHAEL: Susan, for God's sake, shut up.

SUSAN: See what I mean?

MICHAEL: Alf, the whole thing came alive in my head and I just wrote and wrote, feverish, demonic, until it was done. I want to bless the past, brother mine. That's the theme of the play. Reconciliation. I mean, Sophocles, Shakespeare, Chekhov, all good dramatists have been obsessed by it, it's an eternal theme, much in disrepute these days, reconciliation, but I just know this is the perfect moment for it again. It's our story, Alf, the closest brothers you could imagine and how we were driven apart by our different lives, by our –
(*He suddenly winces with pain.* SUSAN *rushes and gets him his vacuum and biscuits. He drinks and eats. He gestures to show he's all right now, smiles crookedly, imploringly at* ALFRED.)

ALFRED: (*Giving nothing away*) What do you want me to do?

MICHAEL: Alf, I want you to see the play. I want you to come to the opening night in five weeks' time, on the 20th of March, you're going to be the guest of honour –

ALFRED: After it's on, you mean? After it's been made public? After the damage has been done, after I've been made a laughing-stock in public? See the play? Before I approve what's in it?

MICHAEL: Don't jump to conclusions, Alf. I'm not out to damage you, no one will laugh at you –

ALFRED: Can't I get through to you, Michael? I'm a private person. I also have a childhood and an adolescence and whatever, I have sons who have private lives and we choose to keep our lives private that's our business, my business, that's my right, you follow me. You put me up on a stage, you make public my life, you're denying me my rights –

MICHAEL: No, no, no, the events, the characters are inspired by our lives but they're transformed, the act of writing transforms them, the act of interpretation transforms them yet again, Jimmy and Derek will transform us. It's like that with all my plays, Alf, they take on another dimension and that's why, I suppose, they're translated, revived all over the

33

place. Take *Family Matters*, it's gone into thirty-two languages, it's playing now, as we speak, in Tokyo and Moscow. That's because it's transformed, it's no longer about you or me or Mam and Dad, it's – it's – well, it's because it seems to be – I'm simply stating a fact – it seems to be universal. Amazing, really. And *Brother Mine* will be exactly the same, the characters are us and they're not us, Alfie, they have their own existence, universal figures, see the play –

ALFRED: (*Gathering strength*) You didn't ask me here for a reconciliation, you asked me here to get my approval, to avoid another lawsuit, you devious, crooked little corkscrew! Mr Jaffey!

(ROBERT *comes to him.*)

Turn on the meter, I want your advice.

MICHAEL: Alfie, wait, wait –

ALFRED: Mr Jaffey, I've changed my mind. I don't want your advice, I'm giving you instruction. Get an injunction!

MICHAEL: Wait, Alfie, wait!

ALFRED: (*To* MICHAEL) You haven't changed. You're only intent on inflicting pain. You're still a self-centred, mega-megalomaniac, you only care about one thing, you, yourself, you. You haven't changed, you little weed –

SUSAN: Please, don't speak to Michael like that, you'll upset him –

ALFRED: Upset him, upset him, I'll upset him, all right. Mr Jaffey! Get an injunction. This man has to be stopped.

ROBERT: Alfred, before we go running to court, I think we should follow your suggestion and read the play first. Michael, let us read the play.

MICHAEL: There's no point. How can I guarantee that the play you read will be the play you see? I can't guarantee that.

ALFRED: Mr Jaffey, don't fiddle-faddle, just get an injunction –

MICHAEL: Alfie, I'll tell you what, I'll tell you what, I'll make a deal, see the play before it's made public. See a preview, a dress rehearsal, I'll arrange a special performance. The actors won't mind, will you, we don't have to bother with Equity or anything like that, just a private performance for Alfie –

DEREK, JAMES *and* SUSAN: Fine, yes, of course, lovely –

MICHAEL: Alf, you'll see the play, privately, then you'll tell me your objections, we'll discuss it, we'll both be reasonable, I'll try to accommodate you. It's important to everyone here, Alfie, that the play goes on. Our lives depend on it, Alfie. (*A gesture to include the others.*) It's important to me, Alfie. Don't censor the play before you know what's in it. We're brothers –

(MICHAEL *controls tears and snivels. Long silence.*

ALFRED *looks slowly from one to the other. Finally, at* JAMES.)

ALFRED: And you, James, I suppose, you play me.

JAMES: No. I play him.

(ALFRED *slowly lets his gaze fall on* DEREK *who becomes deeply embarrassed.* ALFRED *looks at* MICHAEL, *almost imperceptibly shakes his head, is about to go, pauses, returns, takes out his wallet, stuffs a ten-pound note into* MICHAEL'*s hands, turns on* REGINA.)

ALFRED: The dinner's off!

(*And as he marches out taking his coat – blackout.*)

ACT TWO

The same. Four weeks later. Mid-morning although that is not apparent because daylight has been excluded.

Two tables have been set outside the acting area at opposite sides. One is empty; on the other there is an intercom with a microphone, a script, clipboard, papers. MICHAEL *sits at this table, a hunched figure in the darkness.*

A recording of JAMES *and* DEREK *singing 'Me and My Shadow' – ghostly, echoing.*

A light comes on but no one steps into it.

After a moment:

MICHAEL: (*Into intercom*) Charlie, can the song be a pip quieter? And give me just a little more echo, will you?
　　(*The sound is adjusted, the recording played again.*)
　　Good. Set that. Next sound cue.
　　(*Then, over the singing:*)
JAMES'S VOICE: So, here, too, time is meaningless. And age. Age is also meaningless. We, my brother and I, are the age we were, the age we are, the age we need to be.
　　(*The sound of a tennis game. Light changes making it possible to discern a tennis net so arranged that the acting area seems to represent one end of a tennis court.*)
　　But there always seems to be – in my memory at least –
MICHAEL: (*Into intercom*) Right, hold it there.
　　(*The sound cuts out.*)
　　The voice level we set yesterday's fine. But bring the tennis game in more quickly. I wasn't quite sure what it was. And I was wrong about the light for Derek. It should grow. Try to a count of five. I don't like the snap on. Sorry, old darling. Just go back to that, will you?
　　(*He sits, head in hands. While he waits,* SUSAN, *in dressing-gown and a stocking to hold back her hair, enters with vacuum flask and biscuits which she puts on the table. She mouths, 'Have you taken your tablets?' as –*)

36

JAMES'S VOICE: So, here, too, time is meaningless. And age. Age is also meaningless. We, my brother and I, are the age we were, the age we are, the age we need to be.

(ROBERT, *carrying a briefcase, enters, hovers*. MICHAEL *doesn't see him but* SUSAN *does and is uncertain what to do. The tennis game, a little louder. Light grows.*)

But there always seems to be – in my memory at least – a storm threatening. Ominous, a warning – but of what?

(*Sound of distant thunder.* SUSAN *draws* ROBERT *to* MICHAEL's *attention, then hurries off.*)

MICHAEL: (*Into intercom*) That's fine, Charlie. Set lights and sound from the top now. Thanks, Charlie, you're a darling. It's really good. Give me working lights, will you?

(*He clicks off the intercom. The lights go to a working state.*)

Where's Alfred, isn't he coming?

ROBERT: I talked to him on the telephone last night. He was still undecided. If he hasn't arrived by quarter past you'll have to abandon the exercise.

MICHAEL: He'll come. I know my brother. We're very alike. Peas in a pod. Sometimes, when I was writing the play, I thought he and I were the same person. Or simply two aspects of the same person. He inhabited his world and I another. I thought – (*He breaks off, indicates the other table.*) I thought you might like to sit there.

(ROBERT *goes to the table, starts unpacking his briefcase.*)

Where's Regina?

ROBERT: (*Curt*) I've no idea.

(*He sits, settles down. Silence.*)

Michael, may I try out a theory on you?

MICHAEL: Please.

ROBERT: I'm going to have to say something harsh. Alfred's right. You are devious.

MICHAEL: (*Crooked smile*) Is that the theory?

ROBERT: Regina and I had words the other evening. I was batting on about my belief that there is no such thing as coincidence or accident. I do a lot of divorce, you know. And people are forever leaving intimate, compromising letters lying about for their spouses to read – by accident, of course. They just

happen to be hidden under 'his' shirts or 'her' underwear or in a drawer that's supposed to be locked, yet they're always found because they're meant to be found. In the course of our – our discussion, Regina's and mine, she let it slip that you suggested she should put the idea of a surprise party into Susan's head. You told her no more, and left it to her, never mentioned it again. As Regina often says, agents always have to do the unpleasant things for their clients, it's one of her themes. Although she expresses it rather more vividly than that. Now, the question is, why? Why did you want a so-called reconciliation with your brother in front of the rest of us? Why did you want a party in order to tell him about this play? Alfred believes it's because you need an audience – (MICHAEL's *hissed laugh*.)
But I don't. I come now to my theory. It's what I call the Iago complex. You remember what he says? ''Tis here, but yet confused,/Knavery's plain face is never seen till used.' You had a vague idea. Tell Alfred about the play with others present so that perhaps he'd be too embarrassed to make a fuss. Perhaps, you thought, we'd help to draw his sting. Or, as you ventured to suggest, make him feel one of the team, a greyhound in the slips, and so disarm him. But, of course, you didn't disarm him, did you?

MICHAEL: Well, we're not in judge's chambers now, are we? We're not in court.

(*He smiles crookedly. After a moment:*)

ROBERT: You're a shit, Michael.

(MICHAEL *hisses.* REGINA *enters unseen, also carrying a briefcase.*)

It all confirms my view. There is no such thing as accident or coincidence.

(REGINA *ignores* ROBERT *and goes to* MICHAEL. *She kisses him on his cheek.* MICHAEL *immediately senses that she wants to say something unpleasant.*)

MICHAEL: What's happened?

REGINA: The word's out. Nobody's going to pay an advance until this is settled. Nobody wants injunctions flying about. I've talked to the Germans, the Scandinavians, the Dutch.

They're all adamant. No money until this is settled. No doubt I'll have New York on the phone or the fax before nightfall.

MICHAEL: It'll be fine. It'll be fine. Don't worry, don't worry. But you'll have to find me a screenplay. Or a telly. I need cash. Badly. The house in Tuscany doesn't pay for itself, you know. Nor does the flat in Paris.

REGINA: Will you do an episode of *A Thousand and One Nights*?

MICHAEL: (*Sharp*) No, I will not do an episode of *A Thousand and One Nights*. Surely you can find me something more distinguished than that, sweetheart.

REGINA: I'll do my best. Oh, and the BBC called. They want you on *First Preview* tomorrow night –

MICHAEL: Pretentious crap –

REGINA: Autobiography as fiction is the topic. David Tickle in the chair.

MICHAEL: What an asshole. By myself?

REGINA: No, they're getting a novelist, a portrait painter –

MICHAEL: Tell them to piss off, sweetheart. I appear alone or not at all. You know that, they know that –

(*She sits beside him. He starts to look through the script.*)

REGINA: I've left Robert. I walked out.

(MICHAEL *barely reacts. His thoughts are elsewhere.*)

ROBERT: It doesn't look as if my client's going to attend.

REGINA: He's sitting in his car in the car park.

MICHAEL: Why didn't you say?

REGINA: I thought you'd have been told.

ROBERT: I didn't see him –

MICHAEL: Should Regina go down and fetch him?

(SUSAN *enters, wearing some stage make-up now.*)

SUSAN: Michael, the boys are very nervous, I think you should have a word with them, I'm sort of unnaturally calm, what should I do?

MICHAEL: I'll come round and see you all in a moment –

SUSAN: Did you take your tablets?

(*A sudden burst of sound:*)

JAMES'S VOICE: – but there always seems to be – in my memory at least – a storm threatening. Ominous, a warning – but of what?

(*The sound stops.*)

MICHAEL: (*Putting on headphones*) Everything all right? Where's the thunder, Charlie?

(*Sound of distant thunder. While* MICHAEL *listens,* ALFRED *enters in a dark suit. He stands and surveys the set-up. They all see him.* SUSAN *rushes off.*)

(*Into intercom*) If that's easier for you, Charlie, fine. Charlie, are you there? Thank you, old darling. Won't be long now. The audience has arrived.

(*He takes off the headphones and switches off the intercom.*) Good morning, Alf.

(*A sideways nod from* ALFRED.)

ROBERT: We seem to be sitting here, Alfred.

(*A moment's hesitation, then* ALFRED *joins* ROBERT. *He studiously avoids looking at* MICHAEL.)

ALFRED: Mr Jaffey, please be so good as to ask the playwright to whom this Charlie is to whom he is speaking to through that microphone. And please remind him that the conditions he agreed to was that no one else should be present but the participants and the interested parties.

MICHAEL: I'm talking to my electrician who happens to be a genius and who's doing us the great favour of also operating the sound this morning. He's in a box, hidden away, Alf. He's a participant. He's a technician who's a participant. It's all right, I promise you.

(ROBERT *nods reassuringly at* ALFRED. ALFRED *sits.*)

ALFRED: Let's begin, please.

(ROBERT *clears his throat.*)

ROBERT: I'm here in my official capacity as a solicitor, acting for my client, Mr Alfred Manx –

REGINA: Oh, come on, do we have to be so formal?

MICHAEL: As you see, I haven't got my solicitor here. He comes rather expensive.

ALFRED: Who do you think this is? Cut-price Charlie?

MICHAEL: So, Regina's here as my agent. (*He takes the stage area.*) I just want to say something about what you're going to see. (*He paces, turns.*) We all know that Alfred has made up his mind to stop this play no matter what he sees today, but

although I freely admit the play is inspired by real events –

ROBERT: I don't think we want to rehearse the arguments, Mr
Manx –

ALFRED: Right. I came here to see a play, not to listen to speeches
which I've already heard, you follow me.

MICHAEL: Alfie, all I ask is that you give me a fair crack of the
whip. Promise me.

(*No response.*)

We've been rehearsing for a month now, so the performances
are not absolutely ready. But I've deliberately left next week
open to incorporate any changes that – that may be required.
Because of the conditions you insisted on – (*He winces, holds
his stomach.*) Because of the conditions insisted on, Alfie, we
have no stage-hands, so the actors themselves are going to
have to change the scenery, what little bits there are. Now, if
you'll excuse me. I have to see the actors and then we'll
begin.

(*He goes. A long, long frosty silence.*)

REGINA: (*To* ALFRED) My father sends his regards.

ALFRED: (*Icy*) Pat him on the head from me.

(*Uneasy silence.*)

REGINA: Perhaps you should know that this play is not Michael's
usual style, it's cinematic. You should also know that James
Wiley plays Nicky, and Derek Tewby plays Freddie –

ALFRED: Nicky, Freddie, hunh! Manx or Marx?

REGINA: The surname's not specified.

ALFRED: Hunh!

REGINA: Susan plays – all the women.

ALFRED: She plays all the women? Why?

REGINA: (*Dry*) Because this is a fringe theatre.

(MICHAEL *returns.*)

MICHAEL: We're ready. Alfred, I'm going to ask you, for
everyone's sake, not to interrupt. Just make notes. We'll
discuss them afterwards. You're going to love it, Alfie, I
promise you, you're going to love it.

(*He goes to the table, sits. He switches the intercom.*)

(*Into intercom*) All right, Charlie. Let's go. God bless.

(*The stage goes to darkness. A figure,* DEREK, *enters and keeps to*

41

the shadows. JAMES's *and* DEREK's *voices are heard singing* '*Me and My Shadow*' – *the echoing, ghostly recording. A light.* JAMES *steps into it. The two actors speak as their characters, Nick and Freddie.*)

JAMES: This is a play of memory, my memory, but it is not about me. No, the hero of my memory is my brother, Freddie. (*Pause.*) My brother, Freddie, died yesterday.

ALFRED: I don't believe it, he's killed me off before the play's begun. Hunh! Hunh-hunh! Hunh!

MICHAEL: Sssh!

(JAMES *is thrown.*)

JAMES: I've lost it, I'm sorry, I'm awfully sorry, I'm so sorry –

MICHAEL: (*Prompting*) My brother, Freddie, died yesterday –

JAMES: Yes, yes, I'm so sorry –

(*A moment while he collects himself. Then:*)

My brother, Freddie, died yesterday. An urgent call, 'Come quick. Freddie's dying. Make your peace with him.' Nothing provokes memory like a life in jeopardy. (*Pause.*) Memory makes times meaningless. Years, days, decades collapse, expand, develop, coalesce. Memory smashes time, so that it's possible to slip from yesterday to yesteryear as though, in reality, they followed one another, as though memory was one unbroken relevant continuum.

(*The light fades. He exits. The singing continues.*)

JAMES's VOICE: So, here, too, time is meaningless. And, therefore, age. Age is also meaningless. We, my brother and I, are the age we were, the age we are, the age we need to be.

(*The sound of a tennis game. Light grows.* DEREK *has a tennis racket and is miming a hard game against an unseen opponent.*)

But there always seems to be – in my memory at least – a storm threatening. Ominous, a warning – but of what?

(*Distant thunder.* ALFRED *rises, goes to* DEREK.)

ALFRED: Excuse me, excuse me, excuse me, what's this?

DEREK: (*Alarmed*) What's what?

MICHAEL: Alfred, I said you mustn't interrupt!

ALFRED: Excuse me, excuse me, this cannot wait. (*Points at the racket.*) What's this?

DEREK: What? what? I haven't done anything yet –

42

ALFRED: You're holding the racket in your left hand.

DEREK: Yes?

ALFRED: I'm not left-handed.

DEREK: But I am.

ALFRED: Mr Jaffey, will you please note this inaccuracy, this distortion?

(MICHAEL *rises*.)

MICHAEL: Alfred, I'm going to try to make it clear again. These are characters in a play, not you, not me, but characters in a play. The character that Derek plays happens to be left-handed. Is that clear now?

ALFRED: Characters in a play, really, really, yes, yes, I've been thinking about that, you said something of the kind before and I've been thinking about it. If it's as simple as that, if they're just characters in a play, what are we doing here? Why do I have to sit through this charade, if it's as simple as that, you follow me?

MICHAEL: (*Keeping calm*) So that you can understand the exact meaning of what I've just said. What you are going to see is inspired, fed, nurtured by reality but it isn't reality.

ALFRED: Which is another way of saying that you don't have to be exactly accurate either. That's my point, that's what I've been thinking about. That argument gives you licence to do what you like with people's lives. It gives you licence to turn a saint into a cat burglar. Left-handed? I've never been left-handed in all my life. And I'm not dead, thank God. And I'll tell you something else, he has a very short backswing on his forehand. Now, I take the racket right back, you follow me –

(*He demonstrates*.)

MICHAEL: Alfred, let them play the play. We'll discuss the discrepancies afterwards.

REGINA: Please restrain your client, Mr Jaffey. For all our sakes.

(ROBERT *has a whispered word with* ALFRED. ALFRED *settles down*.)

MICHAEL: Sorry, Derek. We'll go back to Jimmy's first voice-over and the sound of the tennis game. Sound cues two and three. (*Intercom and headphones*.) Charlie, did you hear that?

43

(DEREK *takes up his position as the lights go to darkness. Silence.*)
All right, Derek.

DEREK'S VOICE: Yes.

MICHAEL: Right. (*Into intercom*) Thank you, Charlie. When you're ready.

(*A momentary wait.*)

JAMES'S VOICE: So, here, too, time is meaningless. And age. Age is also meaningless. We, my brother and I, are the age we were, the age we are, the age we need to be.

(*The sound of a tennis game. Light grows.* DEREK *again mimes the game against an unseen opponent.*)

But there always seems to be – in my memory at least – a storm threatening. Ominous, a warning – but of what?

(*Distant thunder.* DEREK *mimes serving, running up to the net, jumping, smashing, and then is convulsed with anguish.*)

DEREK: What am I doing? What am I doing?

ALFRED: (*Sotto voce*) Taking your eye off the ball, that's what you're doing –

DEREK: (*Overlapping*) I had the whole court open and I put it into the net. What's the score?

JAMES'S VOICE: Fifteen–forty. Four–five. Match point. To me.

(ALFRED *scribbles furiously.*)

DEREK: You're not supposed to say 'match point', you follow me. It's bad form, Nicky. You're not supposed to say match point.

(DEREK *goes back to serve. Serves.*)

JAMES'S VOICE: Fault!

DEREK: Never!

JAMES'S VOICE: It was a foot out! At least!

(DEREK *takes his time and serves again.*)

Fault! Game, set and match!

DEREK: It was on the line, it was on the line –

(JAMES *comes bounding over the net*)

– you cheat, Nicky, you cheat –

JAMES: I do not bloody cheat –

DEREK: Don't swear at me –

JAMES: Your second service was out by a mile, double fault, double fault –

DEREK: It was on the line, it was on the line, I could see the chalk –

JAMES: You couldn't see chalk if it was on a blackboard –
  (DEREK *leaps on* JAMES, *wrestles him to the ground and starts to lick his face.* JAMES *screams and writhes in discomfort.* ALFRED *chuckles. Blackout in which* DEREK *and* JAMES *rise, and remove the net while* SUSAN *sets a chair.*)

SUSAN'S VOICE: (*Recorded*) Freddie, how many times do I have to tell you? You must stop licking Nicky's face! You must never do it again! Swear on my life! Swear on your father's life! Swear that you'll never lick Nicky's face again!

DEREK'S VOICE: Mam, whose face can I lick then?
  (ALFRED *laughs.* MICHAEL *hisses, hopefully. Light snaps on* DEREK *and* JAMES *putting on tap shoes.*)

JAMES'S VOICE: So it was our mother decided that some activity must be found which we could both enjoy. Something 'creative', she said. I had shown a talent for recitation and attended Miss Sybil Finberg's Academy of Dance and Drama. Freddie, Mam thought, should join me –
  (*Lights grow. Piano music.* SUSAN (*as Sybil Finberg*) *wearing 1950s trousers, shirt, hair in a turban, comes on tapping. She wears a fixed smile of the style and period.* JAMES *and* DEREK *rise.*)

SUSAN: (*As the dance teacher*) Come along, boys, altogether now, shuffle, hop-one-two, shuffle, hop-one-two –

ALFRED: Nothing like, she's nothing like –
  (JAMES *and* DEREK *try to learn the steps.* SUSAN *shows a slightly more advanced step. The boys follow.*)

SUSAN: Freddie, what are those at the end of your legs? Oh! I see! They're your feet. Fascinating.
  (ALFRED *laughs.*)
  Shall we try to lift them, then? Shuffle, hop-one-two-shuffle, hop-one-two-toe-heel-toe-heel –
  (*They dance.* SUSAN *takes* DEREK *aside.*)
  Freddie, I have to say something to you, something very personal. If you want to be Fred Astaire you'll have to lose at least half a stone. You're overweight.

JAMES: He likes cooking and eating, that's why, Miss Finberg –

DEREK: Shut up, you.

SUSAN: Look at your brother. He hasn't an ounce of spare. He's a

45

lovely little boy and if you set your mind to it you could be a
lovely little boy, too. Our bodies are temples, Freddie, we
musn't abuse them, we have to keep them pure –

DEREK: But that doesn't mean I have to eat less, does it? It just
means I can't do ninety-nine-change-hands –

(DEREK *and* JAMES *collapse with laughter.* ALFRED *laughs.*
MICHAEL *looks at him, laughs, too.*)

SUSAN: Freddie, wash your mouth out –

DEREK: Tell you what, Miss Finberg, you teach him, he's such a
lovely little boy. You love him so much, you teach him, leave
me out of it. You're like my mum. Our Nick can't do any
wrong in her eyes, or my dad's. But me? Me? No one gives a
monkey's tit for me, you included.

SUSAN: I will not be spoken to like that. I shall tell your mother
what a rude, insolent –

(DEREK *pretends to throw a fit.* JAMES *imitates him behind*
SUSAN's *back and tries to suppress laughter.* SUSAN *is alarmed.*
ALFRED *laughs with delight.*)

What's the matter? What's the matter with him?

JAMES: He's having a fit, Miss Finberg –

DEREK: Water! Water!

(SUSAN *runs off.* DEREK *instantly comes out of the 'fit'. He and*
JAMES *fall about with laughter. Lights change.* DEREK *grabs*
JAMES.)

You're not going to tell our mum what I did, are you?

JAMES: I will if I want –

DEREK: You won't. You follow me? You won't. I'm not going
back to be taught by that daft cow. So this is what you're
going to do. You'll take the money for the class from Mum –

JAMES: What you up to?

DEREK: You'll take the money for the class as usual, and you'll
just give me my half.

JAMES: Bugger that, I'll keep your half.

DEREK: You'll do what, you'll do what?

JAMES: You heard, I'll keep your half –

DEREK: I'll break your neck, I'll snap it in two –

JAMES: No, you won't because I know about Ariadne.

(*Pause.*)

46

DEREK: (*Shocked*) How do you know about Ariadne?

JAMES: I followed you, that's how.

DEREK: (*Quiet*) You're a worm. You're a devious, underhand, blackmailing worm –

(DEREK *raises his fist.* JAMES *cowers. They freeze. A piano begins to play the accompaniment to 'Me and My Shadow'. Lights change.* DEREK *and* JAMES *start the song and dance,* DEREK *in front,* JAMES *behind as the 'shadow'. But at an appropriate moment, they change places and* DEREK *becomes the 'shadow'.*)

ALFRED: (*Rising*) Excuse me, excuse me, excuse me, what's this? What's this? I was never the shadow, he was always the shadow. Always. He was always the shadow –

MICHAEL: But I'm trying to make a point, an emotional point, it's an image, an expression of what happened, I had this hold over you, I had this ascendency, call it a poetic expression of what happened –

ALFRED: Call it a poetic expression? Are we going to hear the word Art in a moment? Is this where Art comes in, God help us? The moment you say *au revoir* to truth you call it Art? Is this Art?

DEREK: (*As himself; exploding*) I refuse to go on. We're in the trenches here, you know, we're the foot soldiers, we're the infantry, we have to go over the top. We get raked by machine-gun fire, we get bogged down in the mud. It's difficult enough without these constant comments and interruptions. I really do think somebody from Equity should be present –

JAMES: (Sotto voce) Hear – hear –

DEREK: I will simply not go on with this unless that man keeps his mouth tightly shut.

JAMES: (Sotto voce) Good for you, Derek.

(SUSAN, *half changed for her next appearance, peers round to see what's happening.*)

DEREK: (*At* ALFRED) I want to make something absolutely clear. I am playing Freddie in a play not you, Alfred Manx, in real life. I am not trying to imitate you, I am not doing an impersonation or a caricature, I am trying to play the part as written –

MICHAEL: All right, Derek, love, calm down –

47

DEREK: I will not calm down. We are being put through a monstrous ordeal. He has no conception of what actors have to go through. We have to know the lines, the moves, the internal map, the subtext, we have to cope with people coughing and spluttering, and late-comers, God, how I hate late-comers. Ill-mannered louts! If we can be on time why can't the customers? But all that pales into insignificance besides the monstrous, destructive behaviour of this man here. I refuse to go on with this.

ALFRED: I admire you for saying that. You remind me of one of my waiters –

DEREK: Oh, piss off –

(*He exits. Silence.*)

MICHAEL: (*Crooked smile*) Well, thanks, Alf, that seems to be that. I'm sorry, Jimmy, Susan. It's clear we can't go on. Thank you, Alfred, that's what I call a fair crack –

(DEREK *returns.*)

DEREK: What do you mean, we can't go on? We're pros, aren't we, we're being paid, aren't we?

JAMES: (*Sotto voce*) Only just –

DEREK: Of course, we'll go on.

JAMES: (*Sotto voce*) Well said, Derek.

DEREK: Never mind 'well said', what about saying the lines as written? I don't think you've given me one correct cue all morning.

(*A pause.*)

I'm sorry, Jimmy. I'm very sorry. I'm sorry. I'm upset. I'm sorry.

(*To* ALFRED.) I apologize, Mr Manx. It was very unprofessional of me. I'm usually very well behaved, you follow me?

ALFRED: I follow you, Derek, I'm right behind you.

DEREK: But if I could just ask you to let us play these scenes for you without interruption and then, perhaps, you and Michael can argue to your hearts' content. (*To* MICHAEL.) I'm very sorry, Michael.

ALFRED: Derek, I give you my word. Not another sound will you hear out of me.

DEREK: Thank you.

ALFRED: And when this is over, I want you to have dinner on the house at the Café de la Poste. If there's one thing I admire it's a professional.

DEREK: Thank you.

ALFRED: You're a wonderful actor, I slipped in the other night and saw you as Theo, you were wonderful, better than your Planter's Rum commercial –

DEREK: (*Brightening*) Oh? Did you like it?

ALFRED: (*For* MICHAEL's *benefit as well*) I wasn't so keen on the play, I agree with the critics, it's sentimental and it doesn't deal with the issues, you follow me, but as far as you're concerned, I've never seen a man take a part so well. And I look forward to welcoming you to the Café de la Poste.

DEREK: Thank you –

(*He returns to his seat.*)

JAMES: (*Icy*) Are we finished?

(*A gesture from* ALFRED.)

Where shall we go from?

(MICHAEL *consults his script.*)

MICHAEL: Straight on, the street scene. All right, Derek? Sue?

DEREK: Fine –

SUSAN: Yes –

(*While the actors arrange the stage,* SUSAN *disappears to finish her change.*)

MICHAEL: (*Into intercom*) Charlie, we're going to the street scene. That's sound cue – twenty-one. Thank you, old darling.

(*After a moment lights change to blackout.*)

In your own time.

(JAMES *goes.* DEREK *remains on stage. After a moment:*)

JAMES'S VOICE: Shadow. Shadowing. Shadowy. This is the recurring image, the repetitive cast of mind.

(*Light grows.*)

DEREK: (*Calling*) Ariadne! Ariadne!

(SUSAN *enters, playing a whore.*)

I've brought him, Ariadne.

SUSAN: I don't see him.

DEREK: He's hanging about round the corner. He's a bit shy, a bit frightened, you follow me?

SUSAN: Well, go get him, won't you? I haven't got all bloody afternoon. I've got one regular comes at six –

DEREK: (*Very confidential*) I'll pay you now, don't ask him for the money, he's only a lad –

(*He hands over some cash.*)

SUSAN: I should charge double for first-timers, me showing them the way to the stars and all. Well. Where is he?

DEREK: Nicky? Nicky?

(JAMES *enters shyly.*)

This is Ariadne, Nicky.

SUSAN: He's a lovely-looking lad, I'll say that for him –

DEREK: There you are, Nicky, she thinks you're the bee's knees, what did I tell you?

SUSAN: (*Holding out a hand*) Come on, love, it won't hurt –

(*She takes* JAMES's *hand and leads him off.*)

DEREK: (*Calling after them*) And don't forget, Nicky, keep your shoes and socks on. You never know, you can catch athlete's foot in a place like this.

(*He laughs. A few seconds, and then* JAMES *comes running back on, past* DEREK *and off.* SUSAN, *adjusting her dress, returns.*)

How was he?

SUSAN: Quick.

(*Blackout. Sound of* DEREK *and* JAMES *singing 'Me and My Shadow'.*)

ALFRED: That's the first scene with which I have absolutely no objections.

(*Light hits* DEREK *and* JAMES *doing their soft-shoe, but now* DEREK *is in front and* JAMES *is again the 'shadow'. The lights fade. And, as they exit:*)

JAMES'S VOICE: So it was, see-saw siblings, tweedledum–tweedledee, brothers battling for their rattle, waiting for the monstrous crow.

(*Light on* SUSAN *wearing a wig of long, golden hair.*)

ALFRED: If you're talking about a monstrous crow, this'll be my ex-wife Jemima.

MICHAEL: She's called Lilian. Ssh.

50

(JAMES *enters with a tennis racket.*)

JAMES: I couldn't find my brother's racket, Lil. I'll have to teach you another way.

SUSAN: How?

JAMES: I'll show you how you hold it. Take the racket as if you're shaking hands.

(*She does so.*)

Good. Now –

(*Comes behind her, arms round her*) – now, you take the racket back like this –

(*He tries to kiss her.*)

SUSAN: Here, you cheeky monkey –

JAMES: (*Holding her*) I fancy you rotten, Lil, let me kiss you, please, please, I've written a poem to you, Lil, I love you, Lil –

SUSAN: Get off, Nick, or I shall scream –

JAMES: (*Still holding her*) 'No Midas need her golden hair enhance,/For Lilian's gold is hers, her loveliness.'

SUSAN: Stop it, will you, let go –

JAMES: 'And Oberon's drug is powerless to entrance
       The beholder's love-in-idleness.
       In summer's flight – '

(DEREK *enters.*)

DEREK: What's this, then, mixed doubles?

(*They spring apart.* DEREK *approaches* SUSAN.)

You win the prize.

(ALFRED *reacts.*)

SUSAN: For what?

DEREK: For being the prettiest girl I've seen this week –

(SUSAN *is flattered.* REGINA *laughs softly.*)

JAMES: Freddie, I don't need you here, I'm teaching Lilian how to play –

DEREK: So I noticed. Lilian. What a beautiful name. 'You're my Lilian of Laguna, you are my lily and my rose.' Or words to that effect. That's a song could have been written about you –

(*Sound of music for the 'Twist'.*)

JAMES: Fred, go away –

(*A strobe light on* DEREK *and* SUSAN *who start to twist.*)

ALFRED: I'll have to teach him, he's no idea, he's too, young –
  (*Calls out:*) It's like drying your bottom with a towel!
  (JAMES *steps forward as* DEREK *and* SUSAN *dance and exit.*
  Light to a single spot on JAMES. *The music continues.*)

JAMES: I am trying to reconstruct the mosaic of his pain. Each
  tessera, no matter how small, no matter how trivial, is
  indispensable to the synoptical design which is like a
  recurring pattern of my brother's distress –
  (*Sound of a glass being shattered. Sound of people chattering. A*
  drum roll. Silence. A band strikes up Mendelssohn's Wedding
  March. Light on DEREK *and* SUSAN *who wears a bridal veil.*
  The couple beam. Light grows as DEREK *and* SUSAN *sit.*)
  Ladies and gentlemen, we're here today to celebrate the
  marriage of Freddie and Lilian. And, since I introduced
  them to each other, I have been given the honour of
  proposing their health. Now, you all saw Freddie breaking
  the glass into a thousand pieces –

ALFRED: I didn't –

JAMES: – and I want to remind you of what that symbolizes. As
  difficult as it would be to put that glass together again, so
  difficult should it be to part Freddie and Lilian. We all want
  them to be as happy as it is humanly possible to be.
  Personally, I recommend to them the example of our
  parents. Our mam and dad sitting there, hale and hearty,
  thank God, have had, I think it's generally agreed, an
  unusually happy marriage spanning almost thirty years
  because they stumbled upon a secret, and the secret is they
  divide their responsibilities. And they divide them like this:
  Mam takes all the unimportant decisions and Dad takes all
  the important decisions. For example, Mam decides where
  we should live, the size of the mortgage, should Dad open
  another branch of the laundry, where we should go to school,
  and so on. And Dad takes all the important decisions.
  Should Britain enter the Common Market, should Mr
  Macmillan – ?
  (ALFRED, ROBERT *and* REGINA *laugh.* MICHAEL, *irritated,*
  makes notes.)

52

DEREK: (*Suddenly, half standing*) What's wrong with Dad?
    (*All freeze. Light changes.* SUSAN *exits.* ALFRED *makes copious notes. Light on* DEREK *and* JAMES. *Both are crying.*)
JAMES: We're almost orphans.
    (ALFRED, ROBERT *and* REGINA *laugh.*)
DEREK: Nick, Solly Firman came to see me yesterday. He says our dad left a peculiar will.
JAMES: What's that mean, a peculiar will?
DEREK: It means after Mum's been taken care of he left two-thirds of his estate to you and one third to me.
JAMES: What? It can't be true, why'd he do it? –
    (ALFRED *scribbles furiously.*)
DEREK: According to Solly, Dad said you'd have greater need of it, wanting to be a writer, an artist, he said, you'd have greater need.
JAMES: I'm shocked –
DEREK: You're shocked? You're shocked? Hunh, hunh-hunh, hunh! You know what I am? I'm not shocked, I'm short-circuited. Our Dad promised me. He said, 'Don't worry, son,' he said. 'I'll see you have enough to open your first restaurant.' He even said he'd launder the linen for me. At a reduced price.
JAMES: How much did he leave?
DEREK: Sixty thousand pounds.
    (JAMES *whistles, does some mental arithmetic.*)
JAMES: But you'll still have enough to open a restaurant, won't you?
DEREK: To hell with the restaurant, I'm not talking about the restaurant, I'm talking about Dad and you and me. I always knew you were the Golden Delicious in our Mam's eyes, but Dad, I thought, Dad, I thought he was a fair man, a just and honourable man, you follow me. And this is his message from the grave, two-thirds love to Nicky, one-third love to me –
JAMES: Nonsense, it's a practical arrangement, that's all, it's Dad being practical –
DEREK: Practical? Practical? With love you can't be practical.
    (*Quietly; through tears*) Before you were born I was the be-all

and the end-all for Mam and Dad. Never mind the Golden Delicious, I was Pride and I was Joy and I was Pleasure. I was five when you were born, Nicky, and the moment I heard the midwife say, 'It's another boy,' it all soured. Suddenly, there was a miracle child in the house, and me, I was put in grease-proof paper in the larder. I should have expected this. It's the story of my life, you follow me. The milk always curdles.

(*Pause.*)

JAMES: What are you trying to say, Freddie? Are you asking for some of my share? What are you asking, Freddie?

DEREK: I'm asking for nothing.

(*Pause.*)

JAMES: I'm going to try my hand at being a writer. I'm moving to London soon. I need every penny.

DEREK: Why? The fare to London's not so expensive. (*Chuckles; looks for approval.*) Not so expensive –

JAMES: I'll find a room, a flat, and I'll sit and write. I'm giving myself three years. That's why I need the money. I need it to set myself up, I need it to live on. I need a cushion.

DEREK: A cushion I understand, but Dad left you a fully upholstered three-piece suite. I also need a cushion or two, Nicky, you follow me. I've found beautiful premises near St Anne's Square, and Marcel Le Gris, who was at the Poly with me, is going to be my chef, he's a wizard, and we'll give them good French cooking, I'll be maître d'hôtel. Peter Archer, another fellow student, he'll be Head Waiter, we're going to call him Pascal. Lilian wants to keep the books, she's good at figures, but I won't let her, a wife's place is in the home, am I right? I'm calling the place 'Le Bistro', you like that? But if things go badly the first couple of years, I won't need a cushion, I'll need an air-sprung mattress. Dad should've foreseen that, he should have made provision, he should have been fairer, Nicky –

JAMES: Dad saw we have different lives, Freddie, different needs, that's all. My life's bound to be precarious. Yours is settled, assured. I'm sorry, Freddie, truly I am –

(*Lights change.* SUSAN *enters and begins to pace.* JAMES *exits.*

54

DEREK *sits with his head in his hands.*)

SUSAN: I think it's disgraceful –

DEREK: Lilian, I'm in mourning –

SUSAN: I'm in mourning, too, don't worry, I'm in mourning for all the money we didn't inherit –

DEREK: Lilian, please, my Dad's not cold in his grave –

SUSAN: If I had anything to do with it he'd be freezing. How could he leave a will like that?

DEREK: He reckoned Nicky needed it more than me. He's got an artistic bent has Nicky –

SUSAN: Bent, you can say that again –

DEREK: All right, I'll say it again, he's got an artistic bent, bent –
(ALFRED *laughs.*)

SUSAN: How could he do it? How could your own father do this to you?

DEREK: It's unlikely anybody else's father would do it to me –
(ALFRED *laughs.*)

SUSAN: We should go to a solicitor and contest the will –

DEREK: We can't do that. What would people think? We can't make a thing like this public –

ALFRED: Hear hear!

DEREK: Anyway, I don't like solicitors –
(ALFRED *and* ROBERT *laugh.*)

SUSAN: How are you going to open a restaurant? On hay and alfalfa?

DEREK: What's she talking about, hay and alfalfa? I've got enough to open the restaurant. What I don't have is a cushion if the milk curdles –
(*Lights change.* SUSAN *exits. Sound of French accordion music. Background noise of restaurant chatter. Light on* DEREK.)
Ladies and gentlemen, *messieurs et mesdames*, welcome, *bienvenue à* Le Bistro!
(ALFRED *laughs, applauds.* DEREK *bows in 'customers' and shows them to a table.*)
Pascal will be with you shortly to take your order.
(DEREK *mimes going from table to table.*)
Good evening, good evening, everything all right? Thank you, thank you, I'm pleased you're enjoying yourselves.

That's right, I imported Pascal from Paris. May I ask where you've come from? Salford? Really? That far? I'm delighted. Thank you, thank you.

(ALFRED *laughs, applauds.* DEREK *moves on.*)

My Lord Mayor, I'm very honoured you should be eating in my humble establishment. Pascal will be with you in a moment. In the meantime, here's one for you. You can use it in one of your speeches, you follow me. I said to a customer the other night, 'How did you find the steak, sir?' And he said, 'Quite by accident, I lifted a potato and there it was!' (*Chuckles, looks round for approval.*) I lifted a potato and there it was –

(ALFRED *laughs and applauds. Accordion music starts to run a little slow.* DEREK *picks up a telephone receiver.*)

Where's Pascal, I mean where's Peter? What d'you mean he's not there? He's supposed to be at work? He's supposed to be here in the restaurant. I can't be maître d'hôtel and head waiter, can I? What d'you mean, he didn't come back last night? Where is he?

(*Accordion music slower, attenuated, until it grinds to a halt.* SUSAN *enters.*)

SUSAN: He's fiddled us out of how much?

DEREK: Three grand.

ALFRED: And the rest –

SUSAN: Three thousand pounds?

DEREK: Yes, yes, you heard, three thousand pounds. I think.

SUSAN: What d'you mean, you think?

DEREK: I think it may be more.

ALFRED: What did I tell you?

SUSAN: If only you'd have let me keep the books, this wouldn't have happened.

DEREK: He's nicked wine and silver and china. I can hardly lay one place setting.

SUSAN: What are we going to do? Will the bank lend?

DEREK: They're thinking about it. Banks. They're as bad as solicitors.

(ROBERT *and* ALFRED *chuckle.*)

I was wondering if your father –

SUSAN: You leave my father out of it. He's not a well man.

DEREK: I'm not asking after his health, I'm asking after his money –

SUSAN: You leave him be. He's easily upset –

DEREK: So am I!

SUSAN: You should ask your brother for what's rightfully yours –

DEREK: It's ancient history, Lil. It's Nicky's money. I have to find it somewhere else.

SUSAN: You shouldn't let Nicky get away with this. I can't bear him. Arrogant, self-satisfied, self-loving. He's going to give you what's rightfully yours –

DEREK: It's not worth the fuss, Lil.

SUSAN: Go and see him. Ask him for what's rightfully yours.

DEREK: He's in London –

SUSAN: Then go to London –

(*Lights change.* SUSAN *and* DEREK *exit. Light on* JAMES.)

JAMES: The recurring pattern. 19A Foulis Terrace, off the Fulham Road, London SW10, a basement flat.

(SUSAN, *still trying to manage a quick change, enters.*)

ALFRED: Who's she supposed to be now?

MICHAEL: Ssh!

(SUSAN *and* JAMES *kiss. A knock on the door.* DEREK *enters.*)

JAMES: Freddie! Oh God, I forgot you were coming.

DEREK: That's nice –

JAMES: I'm sorry. Freddie, this is Vera. She's a friend of mine. Vera, my brother, Freddie –

(ALFRED *reacts.*)

I'll get some drinks, put some music on. Talk, I won't be a second.

(JAMES *goes.*)

DEREK: You win the prize.

SUSAN: For what?

DEREK: For being the prettiest girl I've seen this week.

(*She is flattered. Soft music.*)

What do you do, Vera?

SUSAN: I work in Soho. I'm a – a go-go dancer.

DEREK: Well. Shall we go-go?

(*They dance. It becomes erotic.* SUSAN *begins to strip.*)

ALFRED: (*Soft, staccato, dangerous*) Stop. Stop. Put on the lights. Put on the lights.
(*But the performance continues for a moment with* JAMES *returning, stopping dead, seeing them* –

JAMES: (*An agonized cry*) Freddie, not again –

ALFRED: (*Distressed*) Stop, I say, stop – (*A roar.*) Put on the lights! (*The actors hesitate. Momentary silence.*)

MICHAEL: (*A whisper; tense*) Working lights, Charlie. House lights. (*Lights change. All eyes on* ALFRED *who rises and advances on* MICHAEL.)

ALFRED: (*Quiet, toneless*) Are you mad, are you totally insane?

MICHAEL: (*Genuinely puzzled*) Alfred, what are you on about – ?

ALFRED: Is that what you're going to tell the world? That I committed adultery in your flat with your girlfriend?

MICHAEL: What's the fuss, Alf? It happened, you can't deny it happened –

ALFRED: What's the fuss? What's the fuss? You're going to show me to the world as an adulterer?

MICHAEL: Alfie, don't be ridiculous, no one cares about adultery these days, people will admire you.

ALFRED: What, for bedding your girlfriend while the wife was in Manchester? They'll admire me?

MICHAEL: Of course, they will, sit down, see the rest of it –

ALFRED: Michael, I think you're seriously deranged. Not everybody lives in your obscene modern world, Michael. I'm a traditionalist, I don't swear, I believe in the family –

MICHAEL: Alfie, what are you talking about? You don't deny you screwed Vera, Elvira, whatever her name was, you were married at the time to Jemima, you committed adultery, what do you mean, you believe in the family? Don't be such a bloody hypocrite. I understand you're a traditionalist because your tradition is screwing a lot of women – (*He hisses.*)

ALFRED: But to put this on the stage, Michael. I have sons!

MICHAEL: They won't give a damn –

ALFRED: But I give a damn, I give a damn. You can't portray me in this fashion. I won't allow it. I simply won't allow it. And to call Elvira Vera. She may be still alive. She may sue –

MICHAEL: No, she won't, I checked, she's married to a
millionaire in Hong Kong, she won't want a scandal –
ALFRED: And she wasn't a go-go dancer. She was a secretary at
the National Theatre. And what's more, Jemima's still alive,
the boys are very close to her –
MICHAEL: What do you care about Jemima, you divorced her –
ALFRED: That is totally irrelevant. Married or divorced I don't
want the world poking its nose into my affairs. Is that clear?
I'm talking about decency, decent behaviour about which
you know absolutely nothing. Because you're an artist,
Michael, above morality, while I'm just an ordinary mortal,
subject to every shame and embarrassment and stricture
society has to offer. Hunh, hunh-hunh, hunh!
(ALFRED *paces like a caged animal.* MICHAEL *tries to keep up
with him.*)
MICHAEL: I meant this play to be a work of reconciliation, Alf. I
promise you, I was hoping to cleanse you, cleanse myself –
ALFRED: You want to cleanse yourself, go have a bath, don't use
me as a bar of soap. Your play, your play, what I've seen of
it, and I can imagine the rest, believe me, your play,
Michael, doesn't bear the remotest resemblance to what
really happened.
MICHAEL: Oh yes, it does, Alfred, it's how I perceived the reality.
ALFRED: Then all I can say is that your perceptions are sub-
standard, second rate, shop soiled. Reality? Reality? You
show me licking your face. You don't tell people why I licked
your face, you follow me? You know why I licked your face?
Because I hated you, Mick, hated you, wanted to kill you,
wanted to boil you in oil. When I licked your face I hoped
you'd die of tongue poisoning.
MICHAEL: I know, I understand –
SUSAN: What nonsense, no one hates Michael! Everyone loves
Michael –
(ALFRED *takes his notes from the table.*)
ALFRED: I've got here pages of inaccuracies. Never mind the
tennis, never mind you never took a set off me, never. Never
mind I've heard that marriage joke at every wedding I've
ever attended –

59

MICHAEL: But that's the point –

ALFRED: And what about Jemima? You could not have got her more wrong. You paint her like a wife who cared for her husband's well-being. Wrong. When you became famous all she ever did was to say, 'And to think I could have married your brother.' I endured years of misery with that cow. And me. Me. Your Freddie. Me. You make me a buffoon. I was never so stupid. I was never so gross. And you, Nicky-Micky, what a heroic figure you come out. Look at James, this fine actor, who portrays you. Could any actor be more wrong for a part? You paint yourself sensitive, poetic, full of feeling. You don't tell that you invited all the family round to hear the contents of Dad's will so that I was too embarrassed to make a fuss. You don't show yourself, when you learned Dad left the bulk of his money to you, you don't show yourself screaming with joy and kicking your legs in the air and saying, 'London! London! Now I can go to London!' You don't show yourself ruthless and devious and cruel, no, not once, never!

(*Silence.*)

JAMES: Can't we continue with the play?

ALFRED: No, we can't continue with the play!

MICHAEL: (*Into intercom*) We're stopping for the moment, Charlie. Take a break –

ALFRED: Take a break? Tell him to take a round-the-world cruise –

(DEREK *cautiously approaches* ALFRED.)

DEREK: May I say something?

ALFRED: Derek, say what's in your heart –

DEREK: Please see the rest of the play. It's rather inspiring, I think, I become a kind of saintly figure, and we've worked very hard on the second act, I have a fine death scene, and Jimmy has a wonderful speech at the moment of reconciliation –

ALFRED: Derek, I want to tell you something. You're a wonderful actor. But I don't care if you end up in the play singing the Hallelujah Chorus as a solo. I cannot, for the deepest personal reasons, which I know you understand, nothing to do with your acting, I cannot allow the play to continue. You're all wonderful actors. Even Susan. Only, Susan, I have to tell you, forgive me for saying this, your portrayal of Jemima, or Lilian as you call her in the play, was very tame. Behind her back I used to call her Muhammad Ali, you follow me?

SUSAN: It's in the writing, then, the writing's very tame –

MICHAEL: It's not in the writing, I've said all through rehearsals you had to be tougher –

SUSAN: Well, I'm sorry, but Jimmy hardly ever gave me the right cue, I was constantly thrown and I haven't got time for the quick change from Lilian to Vera –

MICHAEL: It's always a mistake when husbands put wives in their own plays –

JAMES: (*Attacking*) I was thrown right from the start with all the interruptions. I was thrown at the beginning and I never fully recovered. And I was thrown again when we got a laugh on 'We're almost orphans'! I told you we'd get a laugh on 'We're almost orphans', Michael, I said we'd get a laugh, I really do think the line ought to be changed –

MICHAEL: You've changed enough lines already, thank you, Jimmy, we'll talk about it later –

ALFRED: James, I have no knowledge of whether you remembered your lines properly or not. To me, you were too handsome, too athletic, too sincere, too brotherly. I couldn't believe in you as Michael Manx. It's in the writing.

ROBERT: Alfred – (*Draws him aside.*) Forgive me for being crass, but time is money. What are your instructions? In my opinion I think a judge would grant an injunction.

ALFRED: (*For* MICHAEL's *benefit*) An injunction?

MICHAEL: Hold on, don't let's get excited –

ALFRED: Don't let's get what? Don't let's get what?

MICHAEL: Alfred, you can't make a judgement without seeing the whole play. It's a play written with love. All I can tell you is, that you matter to me, Alf, that's all I can tell you. You matter to me –

ALFRED: Hunh! Hunh-hunh! Hunh!
(*Silence.*)

JAMES: May I say the final speech of the play?

MICHAEL: But there are no lights, no music –

JAMES: Honestly, Michael, it doesn't matter, honestly. Just sit and listen –

(The others sit. The actors collect their thoughts, sit close to each other as if for a word rehearsal.)

SUSAN: I'll give you a couple of lines before –

JAMES: Thank you –

(He collects the script from Michael's table.)

I'm going to read it, I'm not sure I know it.

(He finds the place.)

This is the last scene. Freddie's dying. Nick comes to the bedside.

(He nods to SUSAN.)

ALFRED: Who's Susan supposed to be now?

SUSAN: The nurse.

ALFRED: Thank God, I thought it might be Jemima, I don't want her near me when I'm dying.

(A moment of stillness.)

SUSAN: *(As the nurse)* You can speak to him now but I'm not sure he'll take it in.

(JAMES's reading is flat, unemotional.)

JAMES: *(As Nick)* Freddie? It's Nick. Can you hear me? It's your shadow. It's your brother.

(DEREK moans.)

Don't try to say anything. Just listen. You matter to me, that's all I can tell you. You matter to me. You were, you are one of the most important people in my life. No one ever showed me greater love than you did. Not even Mam, not even Dad, no one. No one ever took greater pride in my so-called achievements. But, in doing that, you were obliged to catch my light. And that was unfair and unjust. You're worth a dozen of me, Freddie. Our separation has plagued me and I know we are both to blame, not just me, not just you. But, please, please, show me a sign of forgiveness. *(Waits; no response.)* We're brothers, for God's sake.

(Silence. JAMES smiles, turns to ALFRED, as himself:)

I just thought it would be helpful, I just thought –

62

ALFRED: It was beautifully spoken, James. Beautiful. Jemima
was right about one thing. When you smile the room lights
up. But, Michael, I've never heard such sentimental rubbish
in all my life. I don't want sentimentality, I don't want false
sentiment, I don't want you to pretend you have love and
admiration in your heart when all you have is cruelty.

MICHAEL: How can you talk about cruelty when all I'm asking for
is understanding –

ALFRED: (*Sudden, explosive*) I understand. Are you happy?
You've got my understanding, here, in front of witnesses, I
understand. Now, I wipe it from my mind, it's in the past,
it's buried, over, forgotten, done with. I understand you,
Michael. Are you satisfied now? Or do you still want to
pillory me?

ROBERT: What d'you want me to do, Alfred? This is costing you
money.

ALFRED: Turn off the meter, that's what I want you to do, turn
off the meter.

(*Suddenly,* MICHAEL *swings round on* ALFRED.)

MICHAEL: You know what, Alfred, you're full of shit, too –

ALFRED: What? What? You turning this on me?

MICHAEL: You just want to find a way of punishing me, of
making my life impossible. Why did you try to stop *Family
Matters*?

ALFRED: You know why, because I didn't want Mam and Dad's
memory sullied.

MICHAEL: Lies, Alfred. You didn't give a damn about Mam and
Dad or anyone else. Listen to the words of my play. 'You
were obliged to catch my light.' What I didn't say was that
you resented it. You resented it and you punished me for a
million imagined wrongs, for coming into the world when I
did. Just admit that you sued me over *Family Matters*
because you were punishing me for simply being your
brother. It had nothing to do with how I portrayed Mam or
Dad. And all your enmity is personal, directed against me
and nothing to do with my plays or anything else. Admit it,
Alfred. You're also full of shit –

(*Deadly silence.* ALFRED *suddenly starts to throw a fit. After a moment,* MICHAEL *imitates him. Then they collapse with laughter, sink to the floor, hysterical.*)

(*Through his hissing.*) You bastard, you bastard –

ALFRED: (*Laughing*) I'm the bastard? I'm the bastard?

(*Their laughter begins to run its course.*)

REGINA: They're insane. My father said they were insane. My father said the whole family was insane.

ALFRED: (*Recovering*) Regina, all happy families are insane, because if they were sane they'd be unhappy, you follow me?

MICHAEL: That's the truth and I tell my truth –

(MICHAEL *embraces* ALFRED *roughly, almost as if they are boys again.*)

ALFRED: Your truth, exactly, your truth –

MICHAEL: But so does every writer who's ever lived. His truth, her truth, my truth, their truth. That's all an artist can do. Take the example of painters. It's easier to understand. Take portrait painters. Just say van Gogh had painted your portrait. It would have been how he saw you, not how you saw yourself. He'd have given your skin an odd-coloured tinge, he'd exaggerate your nose or your eyes, but he'd capture a fleeting, revealing expression which would impart your essence, Alfie, and we'd all recognize that truth. Writing about you is exactly the same, it's born of the same impulse, follows precisely the same process. (*Cajoling, child-like*) You see, Alfie? You wouldn't have objected, would you, if van Gogh had painted a portrait of you?

ALFRED: I would if he painted me with one ear. (*Chuckles, looks round for approval.*) One ear –

MICHAEL: But he'd have conveyed on you immortality.

ALFRED: Thank you for nothing. If I'm going to be immortal I'll wait till after I'm dead.

REGINA: I'd like to say something –

MICHAEL: Regina, this is between Alfred and me, don't interfere, please, there's a good girl –

REGINA: Why mustn't I interfere? Because I'm a woman? Because I'm an agent? Why?

(MICHAEL *turns away.*)

64

What I have to say is very simple and it's a plea to Alfred to let the play go on.

ALFRED: Regina, you have both my ears.

REGINA: I've been a writer's agent for five years. Michael was my first important client, thanks to an introduction made by my father. Since then, I've acquired other distinguished clients. And I've noticed this. The greater the artist the more he covers his agent in shit.

ROBERT: Here we go –

MICHAEL: What d'you mean, the greater the artist the more he covers his agent in shit? Do I cover you in that much shit?

REGINA: (*Dry*) No, not that much.

(*The penny drops.* ALFRED *laughs.*)

All the things the artist most desires but feels would sully his reputation as an artist he heaps in bucketfuls on his agent. His greed, his hunger for fame, his courting of publicity, which, of course, he both wants and doesn't want, his need to feel important, his jealousy of his colleagues, his insecurities, all these things are shovelled on his agent's head. Now, why do you think, Alfred, the agent bears that sort of treatment? Don't answer because I'll tell you. The reason is that the agent, in my experience, believes in art in a way the artist never does. That's ironic, don't you think? I know several of my colleagues, I work with them, and we hardly ever discuss money, or our ten per cents, we discuss only the good of our clients and the true value of their work. Because we believe in their art. Isn't that silly of us? My father wrote an appreciation of Michael for the school magazine –

ALFRED: Yes, yes, I read it –

REGINA: And what did he say?

ALFRED: I can't remember.

REGINA: I'll remind you. In it he said that artists feed the deepest sources of a society's strength. That's what I believe, too. The artist's insight, my father wrote, is a defence against self-deception. The artist can tell you about humanity's suffering and triumph and that's often a help for those who despair. The artist champions the individual and that's not a popular role. Now, Michael, from time to time, writes about people he knows, people close to him. He'll probably write about all this when the time comes. Michael doesn't use his art as a weapon or as a soap-box. He is true to his perceptions and to his gifts and he takes the consequences. If you ask him now why he so desperately wants this play performed he will stammer and stutter because he has such a bad conscience. I assure you it has nothing to do with wanting your forgiveness or performing an act of atonement. He writes because he is obsessed with writing and no more need be said. Think of this play, Alfred, as an artefact, something to be admired or criticized for what it is. Remain aloof. The truth of the matter is, you should let *Brother Mine* be performed, Alfred, because someone may be strengthened and wiser as a result. Perhaps you.

(ALFRED *nods approvingly*.)

ALFRED: Regina, you mention your father. It always amazed me that out of such a small man came such lofty thoughts. You reminded me of his dignity and intelligence. You're your father's child, all right. And for that, the Chocolate Mousse Regina Melnick is back on the menu. The dinner date stands, you name the day. But even so, I have to express a difference of opinion. You see, Regina, I detect that you believe people can change. I don't. And why should Michael want to inflict pain? Is that the function of the artist? To inflict pain? Because this play of Michael's, like all his plays, is cruel. Why should he hold up to ridicule our parents, our family, me? That's cruel. Am I such an unusual man I should be written about, am I such a figure of fun? Why should he degrade me in the eyes of my fellow men, in the eyes of my children? Isn't that cruel? Am I such a terrible fellow he should do this to me, his own brother? No, Regina, the most that can be said of me is that I bear all bravely and my fellow men don't need to know that. I'll tell you what, I don't want them to know. And this is what I don't understand, why does Michael have to write all the time about his so-called roots? Why can't he use his imagination like other people? Where's imagination gone all of a sudden?

66

Isn't imagination the bread and potatoes of art? Where's
imagination gone? Did Shakespeare write about his brother?
No, he used his imagination. Michael should do the same.
Instead of writing about me he should imagine people like
Hamlet or Henry the Fifth.

MICHAEL: (*A mutter*) Hamlet or Henry the Fifth –

ALFRED: No, Regina. You talk about championing the
individual? I'm an individual and what's more I'm a private
individual and my privacy I guard like a lion. And on those
grounds I say no to *Brother Mine*. No, no, no!

JAMES: (*Bursting out*) Oh, please let the play be performed. The
fact is I've been out of work for months, eight months, I
simply haven't worked, I need the money, I –
(*Embarrassed silence.* ALFRED *takes him aside.*)

ALFRED: James, the other day I gave you my card. You've
probably lost it so I'll give you another. (*Gives him a card.*)
Please, I beg you, use the Café de la Poste as your home. Eat
there as often as you like, free of charge. It's not charity, it's
my honour, you follow me. Only, please, don't tell any other
theoreticals, I'm sure you understand.

MICHAEL: (*To* REGINA) I'm not pleased with some of the things
you said, Regina. Sweetheart.

REGINA: Let's have lunch. We'll talk about it.

ROBERT: I have to go. I have a meeting at one. Alfred, what do
you want me to do? Do you want me to get an injunction?
(ALFRED *paces.* MICHAEL *grabs him, tries to swing him round
but winces at the pain caused to his elbow.*)

MICHAEL: Alfred, what do you want? Revenge? You want to
punish me some more? Go on, smash me in the eye, lick my
face, kick me, but for God's sake, don't injunct this play. To
stop this work of mine is like sentencing me to death. I have
very little life outside my work.
(SUSAN *starts to cry.*)

SUSAN: It's true, it's true, that's all he does, I hardly ever see him,
that's all he does, writes, writes, writes –

MICHAEL: Please, Susan. You want to punish me. Injunct the
play. You want to be reconciled with me, sincerely,
truthfully, then allow it to be performed without let or

67

hindrance. I've worked through the material of our lives, Alfie, agonized over it, I know what you've gone through, being my brother, in my shadow, I know, I know. I want us to be friends again. Believe me. But if you injunct this play we'll die estranged. It's up to you, Alfie.

ALFRED: No, Michael. It's up to you. Cancel your play, Michael. Cancel it. Withdraw it. Never mind not putting it on, don't even publish it. Shred it. Pretend it never existed. Let that be the measure of your sincerity. Let that be our reconciliation. You withdraw the play.

MICHAEL: (*Cornered*) Wait a moment, wait a moment, it's not as simple as that –

ALFRED: Oh, yes it is, it's as simple as that, because I'm telling you, Michael, this play of yours causes me pain. You're so keen on a reconciliation, you decide. I give you my word. If you withdraw the play, we'll be friends, we'll be brothers. On the other hand, if you decide to go on with the play, I won't take any legal action, but! You'll never see or hear of me again. If *Brother Mine* is performed, I swear on the graves of our parents, we will die estranged. You want to be reconciled, withdraw your play.

(*Silence.* MICHAEL *paces. He stops, is about to say something, paces again. He stops suddenly.*)

MICHAEL: James, Derek, Sue, let's go into the rehearsal room. I've pages of notes. James, you have to do a lot of work on the lines if you're going to know them properly before we open.

(*He glances at* ALFRED, *shrugs helplessly, starts to go.* ALFRED *strides to him and swings him round.*)

ALFRED: Michael, I'm going to tell you something, because this is the last time I shall ever set eyes on you. You're a ponce, Michael, a scavenger, a bird of prey, worse, because you don't just eat the flesh of the dead, you eat the flesh of the living. You say I lived in your light and I once told you I got pleasure being introduced as your brother. I said there was a kind of glory in that. But we were both wrong because the reverse is true. People should introduce you as my brother because the glory's yours not mine. I learned something today, Michael. You feed off me, just as you feed off everyone you've ever written about. Without me, Michael, you're nothing. That's what I've learned. You live in my light, you follow me. Yes, yours is the glory, Michael, not mine. Not mine.

(MICHAEL *disengages*.)

MICHAEL: Come on boys and girls, we can work until lunch. It all has to be tougher, the sparks have to fly. And James, the last speech. It *was* sentimental, and it needs to be angry. And none of this bogus reality acting, please. I want it theatrically accurate, truthful –

(*He goes.* SUSAN *runs after him.* JAMES *turns to* ALFRED, *makes a small helpless gesture, a wave.* DEREK *hesitates*.)

DEREK: Thank you for what you said about my Theo. I'll do my best for you as Freddie.

(*He goes.* ALFRED *paces, grunts*.)

ROBERT: Can I give anyone a lift?

(*No response*.)

(*To* ALFRED.) We'll talk.

(*He goes.* ALFRED *watches* REGINA *pack up her things*.)

ALFRED: Chocolate Mousse Regina Melnick?

(*She barely glances at him, exits. He stands, lost*.)

MICHAEL'S VOICE: No, Jimmy, no! Don't soften the last line. Let it rip. (*Demonstrating anger*.) 'We're brothers, for God's sake!'

JAMES'S VOICE: (*Yelling*) 'We're brothers, for God's sake!'

MICHAEL'S VOICE: Better!

(*The murmur of their voices. Laughter. The sound of* JAMES *and* DEREK *singing 'Me and My Shadow'.* ALFRED, *a solitary figure, stands and listens. Blackout*.)